A Primer on Christian Worship

Where We've Been

Where We Are

Where We Can Go

WILLIAM A. DYRNESS

William B. Eerdmans Publishing Company

Grand Rapids, Michigan / Cambridge, U.K.

Published 2009 by
Wm. B. Eerdmans Publishing Co.
2140 Oak Industrial Drive N.E., Grand Rapids, Michigan 49505 /
P.O. Box 163, Cambridge CB3 9PU U.K.
www.eerdmans.com

Printed in the United States of America

14 13 12 11 10 09   7 6 5 4 3 2 1

Dyrness, William A.
A primer on Christian worship : where we've been, where we are,
where we can go / William Dyrness.
p.   cm. — (The Calvin Institute of Christian Worship liturgical studies series)
Includes bibliographical references.
ISBN 978-0-8028-6038-5 (pbk.: alk. paper)
1. Public worship.   I. Title.

BV15.D96 2009

264 — dc22

2008051811

Unless otherwise noted, the Scripture quotations in this publication are from the New Revised Standard Version of the Bible, copyright © 1989 by the Division of Christian Education of the National Council of Churches of Christ in the U.S.A., and used by permission.

Contents

Contents

Preface

This brief primer on worship seeks to serve two related goals. First, it seeks to introduce (and sometimes interpret) the current conversations about worship for worship leaders, pastors, and lay leaders. To say that worship issues have become prominent in the last generation would be an understatement. In some circles, worship has become a virtual battleground of competing interests in the church; for others, discussions about worship have constituted a frontier of learning and growth — books, conferences, and periodicals have proliferated that illustrate both dismay and excitement. Though not an expert in the field of worship, I felt it important — partly for my own sake — to try to make some sense of this burgeoning field. I also believed — imprudently, perhaps — that my perspective as a scholar of theology and culture might provide a helpful angle of vision. While the discussion may push the debate in ways that have been overlooked, it makes no pretense at originality. Its primary goal is more modest: to make a very vital conversation about worship accessible to a wider audience. For this reason, footnotes have been kept to a minimum, and questions have been appended to each chapter to encourage conversation and reflection.

But there is a second motivation for the book. While it is certainly valuable to provide a window on what is happening in the field of worship, it is, to my mind, even more important to seek to awaken the average worshiper to the importance of these issues. So this book seeks to encourage deeper reflection on these questions, to the end that we all might become more faithful and biblical worshipers. This in turn touches on a more comprehensive goal: to encourage the process of worship renewal — and the related theological renewal — that has begun in many places.

The treatment I am here able to give the subject of worship has its limitations. I speak much of the diversity of styles that characterize today's churches, but there are other kinds of diversity that I have had to leave to one side. I might have focused more centrally, for example, on ethnic differences, which can no longer be ignored in today's ecclesiastical reality. Though this is surely an interest of mine, I have had to leave to others a consideration of these issues.[1] I have chosen instead to concentrate on the historically significant developments that often cross these ethnic divides.

I am grateful to many colleagues who made this book possible. I would especially like to thank the leadership of the theological students conference of the International Fellowship of Evangelical Students, and especially Daniel Strange, Melinda Hendry, and Robbie Castleman for inviting me to speak on worship at their summer conference in Schloss Mittersill in August 2005. It was the eager questions and discussion at that conference which encouraged me to think that a brief introduction of this kind might be useful. And I would like to thank colleagues at Fuller and beyond who have stimulated me to think more carefully about these issues: Robert K. Johnson; Todd Johnson; Clayton Schmit; Leah Buturain Schneider; John Witvliet; Lester Ruth; Joyce Ann Zimmerman, C.P.P.S.; Karen Ward; Ed Phillips; James Abbington; Ron Rienstra; and Chuck Fromm. Finally, I want to thank my research assistant, Deborah Rogers Bu-

---

1. See Michael Hawn, *One Bread, One Body: Exploring Cultural Diversity in Worship* (Bethesda, Md.: Alban Institute, 2003); and *Gather into One: Praying and Singing Globally* (Grand Rapids: William B. Eerdmans, 2003). See also Cornelius Plantinga and Sue A. Rozeboom, *Discerning the Spirits: A Guide to Thinking about Christian Worship Today* (Grand Rapids: William B. Eerdmans, 2003).

chanan, for help with sources; my editor, Mary Hietbrink; and Jon Pott, who has encouraged this project from the beginning. Though they should not be held responsible for the arguments presented here, this book would not have been possible without them.

July 2008   *San José, Costa Rica*

CHAPTER 1

Introduction: God's Invitation

Worship: God's Work and Ours

Christians believe that the need for worship is deeply rooted in the human personality. Human beings are natural worshipers. Even those who claim no religion at all find themselves honoring, even serving, persons or experiences that they find transformative. Though they would not put it in these terms, they "pay homage" to things that order and give meaning to their lives. These things solicit their continuing and regular attention and, often, their resources. In response, they develop specific patterns of thought and action (the equivalent, perhaps, of creeds and rituals) that help them order their lives. A fulfilled human life inevitably stakes out spaces for devotion.

But Christian worship, though it reflects this human need, is more than simply the human attempt to honor God. Indeed, worship that is rooted in the biblical record does not start with human need or activities at all, but with God and what God has done. According to the biblical narrative, which for Christians is a fundamental source for the forms and practices of worship, God chose freely to create the world and its people. Further, God took the initiative to restore the relationship with humanity when this had been broken from the human side. So the beginning of worship is not some human need but

God's invitation, given first in Israel and then in Christ, to return to God, to be reconciled and healed. Thus the human practices of worship are responses to God's initiative. Even these responses, I will argue, are themselves enabled by the Holy Spirit. Prayer, praise, thanksgiving, and confession are human activities of worship, but at the same time they are also theological sites — that is, places where God is also at work. All true worship has this dual-directional character. God approaches in invitation and blessing; we respond in faith.

Even this preliminary way of putting things has brought us to issues that are deeply theological. Note, for example, how all three persons of the Trinity are actively involved in worship — we are invited by God, in Christ, to respond to divine initiative in a way that is enabled by the Holy Spirit. Later we will spend a whole chapter reflecting on the Trinitarian basis of worship, but here I want to emphasize this two-sided character of worship: Worship is centrally a call and a response. As I have noted, the origin — and eventually the goal — of worship lies with God. Paul's doxology in the middle of Romans puts it this way: "For from him and through him and to him are all things. To him be the glory forever" (Rom. 11:36).

Though worship is always a response to what God has done and continues to do in Christ and by the Spirit, from the human perspective, worship has to do with things human beings do. Though it includes more than this, as we will see, *worship* as we ordinarily use the word focuses attention on what groups of people do together in specific locations at particular times. They gather; they sit, stand, or kneel; they sing, pray, and recite Scripture or the creed. Of course, many of the things that Christians do together in corporate worship are things they also do by themselves or with their families — they have their own personal or family devotions, they pray before meals or before setting out on a trip, and so on. But our focus, for the most part, will be on what Christians do during their corporate worship. Throughout this book we will be asking: What kind of worship does God require of us? What does faithful worship look like?

How Culture Shapes Worship

We will return to God's original calling to worship in a moment, but I want us first to think about the public and social side of our worship practices. We tend to take for granted the way we are used to thinking about worship and practicing it. We imagine that practices familiar to us are somehow normative. Or perhaps, as we have grown up, we have become dissatisfied with our ordinary practices and have adopted another way of worshiping — moved to another church or, perhaps, left the church altogether. In any case, speaking generally, at least in America, we have come to believe that worship in a given church should satisfy our own personal (or family) needs. And if it does not, we will look for a place that does. In other words, worship is invariably *personal*. Again, we suppose this is what "true" worship is about, but this is not necessarily so. Consider our English word for worship. If you look it up in a dictionary, you will find that all the primary definitions reflect this personal (and inward) orientation. *Worship,* the dictionary says, is "reverence," "respect," "devotion," "adulation," and so on. Further down the list you may find a more public and social definition such as "taking part in a religious service." If you look up the equivalent word in, say, a French dictionary, you will immediately see the difference. The closest equivalent is *culte,* whose primary meanings all have to do with public activities and places. The personal character of worship that we Americans take for granted hardly appears. Now we might conclude that this reflects a basic fault in the French religious consciousness, but to do so, I believe, would be a mistake. What it reflects is the fact that religion in general, and worship in particular, necessarily conforms to basic cultural realities.

Worship, then, occupies particular cultural spaces. These spaces issue in unique sets of expectations and encounters. This is not necessarily a bad thing, but neither is it always a good thing. Our American tendency to interpret faith in personal and individualistic terms has a deep history that reflects its Puritan and Reformation past — something we will think about in the next chapter. But this character also reflects its Enlightenment context, in which the individual was

3

understood as autonomous and self-creating. Obviously, we might want to celebrate the former roots while being wary of the latter.[1]

There are many other differences among worship practices than those between the French and the Americans, of course — Catholics and Orthodox will respond differently and come to worship with different expectations than, say, Pentecostals and Mennonites; young Americans come with desires that are different from those of their parents, and so on. Still, each of the patterns that develop, I will argue, is dependent on a common scriptural heritage and a shared, though diverse, Christian history. As theologian Michael Partridge puts it, "[Our many] links are cultivated, and passed on, in the lives of traditions. Innumerable vital patterns for living — and for being a person — are formed (though not completely determined) by imitation and example; by doing as others do . . . by following customs and practices." The performance of faith, Partridge goes on to say, invariably "throws up variations" that become characteristics of various cultures and traditions.[2] This is important to recognize because, to my mind, we have paid far too little critical attention to cultural and traditional patterns. This causes problems either because we fail to see nefarious influences or, equally important, because we fail to take advantage of possible cultural bridges.

We will have much more to say about the influence of our culture as we go along, but the point I want to make here is a theological one. Though they understand this in a variety of ways, Christians believe that their created and cultural situation is not a matter of indifference to God. God, after all, created people out of the dust of the earth to work, eat, and live together in families and communities, and by their corporate and embodied lives to bring glory to God. Indeed, in the Incarnation, God chose to become a part of the physical order and, by his death and resurrection, to redeem and re-orient that order. More-

1. I have sorted these roots out in more detail in *How Does America Hear the Gospel?* (Grand Rapids: William B. Eerdmans, 1989).

2. Michael Partridge, "Performing Faiths," in *Faithful Performances: Enacting Christian Tradition,* ed. Trevor Hart and Steven Guthrie (Aldershot, Hampshire, Eng.: Ashgate, 2007), p. 77.

over, in the New Testament, God calls believers into a particular cultural space that is called the church (literally, "those called"). The activities that make up what we call worship — prayer, praise, song — constitute some of the highest pursuits of which human beings are capable. And they involve participants totally, with the whole of their bodies and their minds, their wills and their emotions. The space of the church that we call worship is not inert or abstract; it is charged with the presence of God. Therefore, people who come into this experience cannot remain passive or indifferent. The spiritual space of worship "puts them into play," much as the space of a game puts people into play.[3] It is in this sense that we can say that the practices of worship are theological practices.

Not everyone who comes to church has the same level of comprehension about this theological backdrop. Indeed, a complete articulation of the theology that underlies worship, even if such a thing were possible, is not a prerequisite to engaging in worship. God's invitation to worship is extended to all alike, whether learned or simple. To be sure, everyone who prays or gives thanks must understand something about God — that God is Creator and Sustainer and the Giver of All Gifts. Moreover, faithfulness in worship is a great teacher of theology, as I will argue. But the reverse is not necessarily the case: theological insight does not in itself guarantee true worship. This way of putting things may seem strange to readers who, as we noted above, are used to hearing that God only cares about what is going on inside our hearts and minds.

The Importance of Focusing on Worship Practices

A focus on worship practices is important because they are the common heritage of Christians in all places and times — they are what bind Christians together with each other and with God. Moreover,

---

3. I owe the expression "puts us into play" as a description of worship to conversations with Troy Bronsink.

this emphasis on the usual practices of worship also reflects the actual relation between theology and practice. We begin with the practices of worship because they are logically (and often historically) prior to the development of well-defined theological positions. This truth is reflected in the ancient conviction of the church that worship is "primary theology." The language of prayer, praise, and confession is the fundamental language of the Christian faith. Formal theological language always builds and reflects on this language of worship. As the late theologian Catherine La Cugna explains,

> The language of praise is the primary language of Christian faith, and for that reason the liturgy is sometimes called "primary theology." Primary theology takes place at the point at which God touches us through word and sacrament, and we in response offer thanksgiving, supplication, invocation, benediction to God. . . . The worship and praise of God is the living context, the precondition even, for the theological enterprise.[4]

What is formally called "theology" is, then, a secondary reflection and elaboration of the life of worship and prayer that provides the warp and woof of the Christian life in all places and times.

This priority of practice means that a person's prayer may be a better indicator of her beliefs than her explicit statements of faith. Show me a person's practice of prayer, and I will show you her theological convictions. Prayer indicates not what people *say* they believe but what they actually *do* believe — and believe in such a way as to act on it toward God. Prayer, along with praise and confession, expresses believers' core convictions about themselves and the world. (The reverse is true as well, as J. J. von Allmen points out: What cannot be translated into prayer is probably bad theology.) In the ancient church, this idea was articulated in the Latin expression *Lex orandi, lex credendi* — that is, the church's prayer sets the pattern for its belief, which is to say that belief is ordered by prayer, not the reverse. A

---

4. Catherine M. La Cugna, *God for Us: The Trinity and Christian Life* (San Francisco: HarperSanFrancisco, 1991), p. 357.

deepening life of prayer strengthens one's faith. If this is so, then encouraging a more thoughtful practice of worship, the goal of this small book, may be a good way — perhaps the best way — to further believers' theological maturity.

But throughout the discussion here we will be using *practices* in a particular way — to refer to those communal activities whose purposes and goals have been developed over long periods of time. Such activities are not limited to religion, of course. In the political arena, for example, voting is such a practice, with a long history and a deep meaning. Even if people may not, in a particular election, give a great deal of thought to the activity of voting, they engage in a practice that has wide historical and social ramifications — that power, for example, resides with people and not only with leaders, that each person has the same opportunity to express opinions, and so on. Sociologists and philosophers speak of such practices as "theory laden" — that is, having deep and intrinsic meaning. And this expresses a further reason for our emphasis on practice. The habits we emphasize are "thick" practices, in that they often involve layers of meaning, all of them involving in some way human response and relationship to God. We may also speak of such forms as symbolic, as transparent to a transcendent reality that gives them meaning — in this case, to the activity of God. So, although we begin with the practices of worship, we do not thereby leave God out of account, for these activities are themselves theological matters.

The Relationship between Scripture and Worship

The priority of worship practices is evident not only in the history of the church, but also in the Scriptures themselves. Biblical scholars in various ways have argued that worship is fundamental to the narrative of Scripture. This is true not only in the sense that the narrative includes accounts of worship and instructions about true worship, but also in the sense that the material of worship itself — the songs, the litanies, the confessions — frequently provides much of the content of biblical writings, both in the Old and the New Testament. Indeed, some scholars have argued that worship not only constitutes the goal of the story — as the book of Revelation makes clear — but in many cases provides structure for the story itself.

One example of such an approach to the biblical materials is a recent study of the Pentateuch (the first five books of the Bible) titled *The Torah's Vision of Worship* by Samuel Balentine. Professor Balentine argues that the Torah is structured by a particular vision of worship. For Israel, responding to God's call to worship, as this is conveyed in the Torah, represented "the principal means by which [this] community of faith . . . attain[ed] clarity about God, God's design for the world, and the role of humankind."[5] This orienting vision is reflected in the way these books are structured — at the beginning, with a collection of narratives coming from the creation; in the middle, with instructions about worship and the tabernacle (Exod. 19–Num. 10); and at the end, with stories about the journey into the Promised Land. At the beginning, the creation account is structured as a "liturgy of creation," which Balentine believes is a liturgy of order rather than of origin. This probably grew out of a litany that was a central part of Israel's worship. It is a "summons to celebrate and participate in the ordered, ritual, and relational world that God calls into existence."[6] Because this cosmic order is fragile, as the early chapters of Genesis make clear, God had to establish an everlasting covenant that reaffirms this order. This covenant, expressed in the deliverance of the Exodus, is embodied in what Balentine calls the liturgy of the covenant. Israel is called to express this covenant ritually through the ordered spaces and actions outlined in Leviticus, which is pointedly at the very center of the Torah. In the building of the tabernacle and by their ordered obedience, Israel is engaged, Balentine believes, in acts of "world construction."

In Deuteronomy the attention is turned toward the future, when

---

5. Samuel Balentine, *The Torah's Vision of Worship* (Minneapolis: Fortress, 1999), p. 4.

6. Balentine, *The Torah's Vision of Worship*, p. 81.

Israel will inhabit the land God will give them. Especially in the Covenant of Moab (Deut. 29–32), Israel focuses on the choices that lie in front of them. These choices again are affirmed in worship, which "imaginatively [creates] a new world in which God's cosmic design may be more fully actualized."[7] Worship, then, enabled God's people not only to affirm and celebrate the created order but also to respond to God's creative work by constructing a just and righteous community in the land God would give them.

Notice how this reflects the dual directionality of worship that we noted earlier. God creates a world that reflects the divine wisdom and calls a people to respond to this loving initiative; Noah, Abraham, Sarah, and Moses respond by instituting rituals of worship. Moreover, this worship motivates and sustains the people's community formation. Balentine concludes, "The act of worship is an extension of God's creative work into the community-building and world-building that upholds the order of creation."[8] Worship on this view is grounded in the creative acts of God, both in creation and in the Exodus, which precede and enable the human response. The answer of worship embodies these realities and becomes itself an act of "world construction."[9]

Throughout the remainder of the Old Testament, the activity of worship always refers back to the mighty work of God in the creation and the deliverance from Egypt. In particular, the actions of the priests consistently represent these mighty actions. Old Testament scholar John Kleinig describes temple worship as it is portrayed in the books of the Chronicles:

> Through the ritual performance of choral music during the oblation of the burnt offering, the singers presented the Lord to his assembled people. They evoked the Lord and announced his presence to the congregation . . . they spoke for God to his people. As they sang their songs of praise, they announced the Lord's accep-

7. Balentine, *The Torah's Vision of Worship*, p. 215.
8. Balentine, *The Torah's Vision of Worship*, p. 68.
9. Balentine, *The Torah's Vision of Worship*, p. 34.

tance of his people and declared his favorable disposition to them; they also proclaimed the Lord's deliverance of his people and secured his intervention against their enemies.[10]

Notice how the very acts of worship, the singing and praising, reflected and represented God's very presence among the people. Invited by God, this praise became itself a divine garment.

The New Testament continues this emphasis on God's initiative as it is seen in the life and work of Christ. Christ becomes our Passover Lamb, who, like the Old Testament priest, shows forth the glory of God to those with eyes to see. When Jesus tells the woman at Jacob's Well in John 4 that "the hour is coming, and is now here, when the true worshipers will worship the Father in spirit and truth" (John 4:23), he surely meant for her to understand this in the context of his promise to give her "living water." What he surely did not mean is that worship will now — in contrast to Old Testament worship — become a purely internal and mystical affair (a widespread interpretation that reflects our unique cultural situation). John's Gospel is filled with liturgical and Eucharistic motifs, including the wine at the marriage in chapter two and the water at the Festival of Booths in chapter seven. As believers are led by the Spirit to respond to Christ, to worship, they will be led into all truth, as John says later (John 16:13). The rituals of their worship will be shaped by this new and living Word of God, Jesus the Christ.

Just as worship may have structured critical parts of the Old Testament, so it was critical to the development of the New Testament. In an important article, theologian Daniel von Allmen argued a generation ago that it was within the practice of worship in the early church that theological reflection was born. Quoting Edmund Schlink, von Allmen notes that "the basic structure of God-talk is not the doctrine of God, but the worship of God."[11] The early church began its life by

10. John W. Kleinig, *The Lord's Song: The Basis, Function, and Singing of Choral Music in Chronicles* (Sheffield: JSOT Press, 1993), pp. 180-81. I owe this reference to Jeremy Begbie.

11. Daniel von Allmen, "The Birth of Theology: Contextualization as the Dy-

singing its faith, and some of its hymns are recorded in the New Testament. This process, he argues, began as a spontaneous response to the missionary situation in which the Greek-speaking Christians found themselves. They translated *Lord* as *Kurios,* which was the term applied to the Roman emperor, as a way of making their worship intelligible to Greek-speaking believers. They did not create the narrative itself, of course — as von Allmen notes, they pointedly avoided changing the preaching tradition they received (1 Cor. 15:1-3).[12] Rather, their creativity was expressed in the development of their worship. Their hymns included adaptations of Old Testament materials and original poems. In perhaps the most famous worship song of all, they put Isaiah 45:22-23 into poetic form for their new situation:

> Let the same mind be in you that was in Christ Jesus, who, though he was in the form of God, did not regard equality with God as something to be exploited, but emptied himself . . . and became obedient to the point of death . . . so that at the name of Jesus every knee should bend, in heaven and on earth. (Phil. 2:5-10)

This early Christian hymn recalls the argument of Balentine. He insists that worship mediated Israel's affirmation of the cosmic order in creation with their call to form a community that would bless the nations. So here in Philippians, Paul uses this hymn to connect their call to be "of the same mind" (2:2), both in their community formation and in their worship of Jesus. Moreover, this "Lord" is the same "Jahweh" that in Isaiah 45 calls all the ends of the earth to "Turn to me and be saved" (Isa. 45:22). Thus, von Allmen argues, the early Christians reordered their cosmic structure first in their practice of worship; theology came later to provide a critical, ordering function. In their response of worship, they first expressed the new order of things that Christ had introduced (which, incidentally, Paul says they could not do without the Holy Spirit speaking through

namic Element in the Formation of New Testament Theology," *The International Review of Missions* 64 (January 1975): 41.

12. von Allmen, "The Birth of Theology," pp. 41-42.

them; see Romans 8:15, 26). Here too, interestingly, they were at the same time contextualizing the Gospel message for a (new) Greek audience. The centrality that practices of worship enjoyed in Scripture, and in the early church, suggests to us that these practices should also be central to our lives as twenty-first-century Christians — and that careful and thoughtful reflection on these practices is part of the way our minds and lives will be conformed to the likeness of Jesus Christ.

The Approach This Book Takes

The preceding reflections determine the approach that this book takes. The point of view taken in the discussion will be that of a Protestant in the Reformed tradition. Though Protestant and broadly evangelical, it will also be ecumenical. And this latter fact calls for some comment. I have felt it important to emphasize the ecumenical character of worship for two reasons. First, the discussion in the next chapter will sketch out the long connection that modern worship displays with the classical, medieval (and therefore Catholic) traditions of Christian worship. It is the argument of this book that these ancient traditions, whether closely or loosely followed, still inform the practices of Christian worship today. And, more importantly, this rich tradition has the ability to renew our contemporary worship; the issues this story raises continue to dominate our discussions of worship. Second, the argument here also assumes that much of the current renewal of worship has been influenced (sometimes unknowingly) by the liturgical renewal within twentieth-century Catholicism. From the first decades of the twentieth century through the important years of the Second Vatican Council (1961-1965), Catholics have been engaged in transforming their rich tradition in ways that make it more accessible to contemporary worshipers. This process, while it has sometimes learned from Protestants, also has much to teach them. Indeed, the process of learning is a mutual one. Since Vatican II, Catholic worship has adopted practices that long flourished in the Protestant traditions.

Since then, Protestants have gained immensely from a rediscovery of ancient (Catholic) practices.

While I will recognize the different forms that worship has taken and the (sometimes acrimonious) tensions and conflicts these differences have caused, my goal will be to explore the common ground that all Christian worship shares. A further goal will be to show the ways in which contemporary differences are more about culture — what I will call "style" — than about historical and theological substance, though implications for these are not absent altogether. My hope is that when worship differences can be seen in their particular historical and cultural setting, ways may be found to understand and perhaps appreciate how these differences represent attempts, more or less successful, to contextualize worship in such a way that mutual learning can take place.

A Note on Worship and Today's Media Culture

We have reviewed some of the biblical evidence for the importance of worship in the life of Christians, and noted that worship is currently experiencing a renewal in many parts of the church. Unfortunately, there is more to be said about the current state of worship — which may constitute a final and critical reason for a book of this kind. There are powerful cultural currents that seem to be working against any sustained renewal of worship, even among serious Christians. While these will be discussed in further detail subsequently, they should be acknowledged here. Not only are current trends critical to any discussion of worship; my argument will be that the renewal of worship today depends in important ways on the church's response to these cultural realities. Consider two examples — two disparate issues that, on reflection, turn out to be related not only to each other but also to any renewal of Christian practice.

First, there is the dominance and accessibility of the media that seek both to rival and to influence the practices of worship. Movies, television, and related media rival worship in representing forms of life that embody other (economic or ideological) allegiances. For many people today, engagement in popular (or elite) culture has become a kind of substitute religion, complete with its own myths and rituals. But, as I argued above, these cultural products are neither uniformly hostile to nor unfailingly supportive of Christian worship. In their ability to manipulate and arouse, strong media images can encourage hedonistic self-indulgence, but they can also portray the human situation in powerful ways. The power of these images can become addictive and distracting. But these same qualities can also be used to serve more substantial values and practices — indeed, they often embody forms of great spiritual potential and great beauty. What is certain is that popular media culture has caught the attention of this generation. For these reasons, the media in various forms have inevitably found their way into church sanctuaries. Here they can serve the liturgy, but they can also subtly subvert it. The danger in the entertainment culture is that it encourages a superficial and often passive response to material. It can discourage deep reflection and encourage quick fixes for deep-seated human problems. We may see ourselves and our children mirrored in an episode of *Two and a Half Men* or in a movie by Denzel Washington, but we are seldom encouraged to see this life within a larger, transcendent framework. Paul Griffiths describes our consumerist culture as endorsing a kind of reading "bent on extract[ing] what is useful or exciting or entertaining from what is read, preferably with dispatch, and then [moving] on to something else."[13] Worship, by contrast, encourages slow practices that feed the deep hungers of our hearts.

But there is a further, not unrelated cultural reality that I want to emphasize, which might be summarized in this way: Today's youth-oriented culture is in love with spirituality but distrusts religion. While the formal and institutional aspects of religion (and, for that matter, many other forms of civic life — including voting!) seem increasingly irrelevant, especially for younger people, the search for

---

13. Paul Griffiths, *Religious Reading: The Place of Reading in the Practice of Religion* (New York: Oxford University Press, 1999), p. ix, quoted in Mark Burrows, "To Taste with the Heart: Allegory, Poetics, and the Deep Reading of Scripture," *Interpretation,* April 2002, pp. 172, 173.

spiritual reality and deep encounters with God and others is more intense than ever. This presents Christians with a serious challenge and a crucial opportunity. For worship, while it *expresses* spirituality, is necessarily *embodied* in religious forms. While worship calls forth deep feelings, it is finally not an individual quest for an encounter with God or the spiritual. Worship orients itself around particular things that God has done in history, and it is primarily about things that Christians do together in the presence of God.

The question becomes insistent: Why do the common practices of worship often seem irrelevant today? The problem is often laid at the door of this unreflective generation, which prefers a free-floating spirituality to traditional forms of any kind. Of course there is some truth in this charge, and if this were a book about apologetics and evangelism, I would perhaps focus on this weakness. But what if, in part, the problem is with the state of these practices? What if, under the influence of the functional literalism of our consumerist culture, the church's forms have become barren and opaque — what if they are no longer transparent to their ground in God?

Throughout their history, the forms of Christian worship, at their best, have been resonant with the spiritual presence to which they refer. They have often been shaped into music or art of lasting beauty. Their vitality has not only nourished Christians in their faith, but has also often served to renew forms of the larger culture as well. What if the tensions and struggles we are facing today in the church represent a providential opening to recover this spiritual resonance? Christian practices of worship are often criticized today because they are captive either to simple traditionalism or to the simplistic search for new and entertaining forms of expression. In either case, there is the healthy recognition that these forms *ought to be* critical carriers of spiritual power. What is needed is a recovery of an understanding of Christian worship as providing symbolic resonance and theological depth. If this were to happen, the symbolic depth of Christian practices might provide a winsome contrast to the superficial culture of entertainment that surrounds us, even as it also satisfies the spiritual longings of our contemporaries.

I have argued that worship inevitably reflects its cultural context. And in this respect it faces two perennial challenges. On the one hand, while it draws its nourishment from the story of the Gospel that has been received from Scripture and tradition, worship has to confront the false gods and facile desires of its context. But on the other hand, while it must not conform itself to this world, worship has always to situate itself within that world, finding its voice in the language of the day and in its genuine spiritual longings, even as it presents a rhetorical vision of an alternative world that God in Christ is bringing into being. The challenges represented by this dual calling represent the substance of the chapters that follow.

QUESTIONS FOR DISCUSSION

1. What do we mean when we say that worship practices are "theological"?
2. Since worship is dual-sided, something that happens between God and believers, do you think a good way of thinking about the worship experience might be as a "conversation between us and God"? What might be the strengths and/or weaknesses of such a model?
3. What are some specific ways in which your culture affects (or infects?) the way you worship? Discuss this as a problem and as an opportunity.
4. Discuss other "worship practices" in the New Testament that might be considered places of theological innovation (see, e.g., Matt. 3:13-17; Acts 2:4; Acts 4:32-33).
5. Discuss the problems and opportunities provided for worship leaders by the media, especially the movies, and popular culture.

CHAPTER 2

Looking Back

Worship in the Middle Ages
and the Reformation

Contemporary discussions of worship, I'm happy to say, are beginning to pay attention to the patristic (relating to the fathers and mothers of the early church) background of worship as well as its medieval background.[1] There is a growing recognition that we have a great deal to learn from reflection on this period of worship history. In the introduction I noted that a challenge today is to recover forms of worship that resonate with cultural hungers, while maintaining their biblical and historical integrity. This challenge is not new. From the time of the New Testament, Christians have struggled to make their witness and their worship both faithful and pertinent. In this respect, the medieval background of Christian worship provides a particularly interesting case study — for two important reasons. First, it was during the Late Middle Ages that a consensus was reached on the general structure of worship. Hundreds of years of struggle over appropriate contemporary forms of biblical worship led medieval Christians to a general outline of worship that, against all odds, has had enormous influence on worship ever since. A second important reason for paying some attention

---

1. The late and lamented Robert Webber has been a leading voice in calling attention to the ancient roots of worship, among other things. See *Worship: Old and New* (Grand Rapids: Zondervan, 1994).

to the medieval period is that, within this general structure, a great many forms of devotion flourished that were subsequently challenged (and often abolished) during the Reformation. While the general structure of worship remained influential, much of the texture and detail was lost, at least to Protestants. Indeed, it would probably be difficult for a medieval person to recognize the continuities if he or she were placed in the middle of a contemporary Protestant service.

There were good reasons for the reformation of worship that occurred in the sixteenth century, of course, and I will briefly describe some of them. But there is also good reason to feel, in retrospect, that while much was gained, some things were lost. Moreover, what was lost — what can be summed up as culturally significant symbolic practices — might well have a contribution to make to the current controversies about worship. It is clear from a reflection on this period that most, if not all, of the discussions and debates that we engage in today are rooted in issues that were first raised in the medieval period. This in itself is reason enough for a brief sojourn in this period.

It is probably difficult for the many tourists visiting famous French and Italian cathedrals today to imagine what medieval worship was like. One can see something of the physical setting of worship, but the actual experience of worship in the fifteenth century is harder to recover. We do know that medieval worshipers inhabited a unified universe that was symbolized in both the church structure and the activities that went on inside. Even today, wherever one looks in a Gothic cathedral, one can see stories of Scripture or images that make visible the story of salvation. In the fifteenth century these physical reminders would have been supplemented by the many ceremonies of the liturgy and the feast days led by priests in elaborate robes. In contrast to worship in many contemporary churches, where quiet worshipers sit in neat rows, medieval worship would have seemed a disorderly affair, with noisy crowds milling about the open space of churches, waiting anxiously for the moment in the service when the priest would hold up the wafer and call out *"Hoc est corpus meum"* ("This is my body").

For people of the Late Middle Ages, the experience of worship would not have been limited to the inside of churches. Its practices would have spilled into the streets as processions wound their way through the town during feast days, or onto the roadways as pilgrims made their way past roadside shrines to Rome or Compostela. Images of saints and biblical characters would have been visible everywhere — in public places and in private shrines at home. We also know that, for most people, faith was largely implicit, as priests struggled to get their mostly illiterate parishioners to learn their "Our Fathers" and reflect on the seven virtues or the seven deadly sins.

Since the educational achievement of most parishioners was limited, there would have been much that medieval worshipers did not comprehend, beginning with the Latin language of the mass. Reformers, both in the sixteenth century and before, worked to raise the level of understanding and participation. But the basic contour of worship — the mass, the processions, the yearly confession and communion, the many feast days — would have been very familiar to everyone. Indeed, these events structured their corporate lives. They lived their lives in the assurance that this faith and these practices would protect them from the only certainty they knew, sculpted over the main entrance of every cathedral: death and the Last Judgment.

The Symbolism of Medieval Worship

The comfort that medieval people derived from worship related to the way they understood the world as a unified dramatic process leading from birth to the grave, a drama that was reiterated week by week in the mass. After centuries of development, this drama took the form of a liturgy — literally a work of the people, practices and responses by which they sought to meld their lives into the dramatic events of Christ's life. The people's understanding, while it should not be exaggerated, should also not be belittled. For it rested on clear actions and ceremonies that held deep, if unarticulated, meaning for them. It rested, for example, on certain specific *symbolic actions* of the priest during the mass.

These actions had ancient patristic roots, but came to their ordered form in the thirteenth century. Already by 1140, chant-texts read by the priest laid out specific prayers following the introit (or the first approach of the priests to the altar). These parts were called the Gloria, the Credo, the Sanctus, and the Agnus Dei, after the first Latin words in these prayers. Somewhat later, this worship came to be specifically ordered. Albertus Magnus, Thomas Aquinas's famous teacher, saw three parts: an introit, up through the first general prayer (called a "collect" because it collected all the prayers of the people together); an instruction through the Credo (or the recitation of the creed); and an oblation, which focused on preparation for and celebration of the Eucharist.[2]

After about 1200, the drama of the mass came to focus on the gesture of the priest raising the host, signaling the moment when it was converted into the body of Christ. While all the senses were called into play in medieval worship, this climactic moment underlines the centrality of sight in it. People needed to *see* the host, and they would push and shove to get a better view, calling out, "Lift it higher." Simply the sight of the raised host at this critical moment, it was believed, conveyed special powers (an event that was called "ocular communion"). Many other actions — "sacramentals," as they were called — held significance: the use of incense, the sprinkling of holy water, the pronouncement of blessing and absolution by the priest, all of which contributed to the dramatic character of worship.

Besides these special actions, there were *objects and images* that represented the significance of the worship experience. The host itself was central, but this centrality was frequently supplemented (or threatened) by veneration paid to various images and relics of the saints. The latter were often placed beneath the altar and carried in procession around the town during feast days. These relics represented a sacred presence that lent gravity to the experience of worship. The tabernacle and reliquaries, which contained the host and

2. See J. A. Jungmann, *Mass of the Roman Rite,* trans. Francis A. Brunner (London: Burns & Oates, 1959), pp. 80, 86.

the relics, became significant objects of veneration and frequently were made into beautiful works of art. The church building itself was a kind of comprehensive symbol, with its large entrance below a portrayal of the Last Judgment; its images of biblical figures and the church's patron saint; and the altar itself, often with an altarpiece raised behind it — which, when the altar was moved away from the back wall in the twelfth century, became the first instance of panel painting in Western art. For the medieval person, all of these things together would have represented what we today call the media. The church would have been the unique site of beauty and drama, an economic center where goods were stored, even the place from which the news of the day would have been disseminated.

Modern persons reflecting on medieval worship, especially those shaped by the Protestant tradition, are likely to see sacramentals and images as symptomatic of how medieval believers had lost their way. Clearly, the use of these objects was subject to abuse, especially later in the period, as we will see. But most medieval believers would likely have been surprised at the charge of idolatry often levied against the use of religious images. They were taught to honor these images as appeals to prayer (both to the saints represented and, through them, to God) and even as sites where God's grace was specially available — but theologians consistently stipulated that these were to be venerated, not worshiped. For medieval worshipers, these objects had spiritual depth; they facilitated rather than obstructed the presence of God. According to noted historian Carlos Eire, at the end of the Middle Ages "the belief in the objective presence of the divine in material elements could not have been intensified much further."[3]

The change represented by the Reformation in this respect could not have been greater. For the medieval worshiper, the world was filled with what were called "vestiges of God." Objects and events could at any moment become a carrier of spiritual reality. For the major Reformers, by contrast, the world could not hold God, and places

3. Carlos M. N. Eire, *War Against the Idols* (Cambridge: Cambridge University Press, 1986), p. 17.

and actions that could transmit spiritual truth were greatly reduced — with obvious and long-lasting implications for worship. During the Reformation, the practices of pilgrimage and the veneration of images came under particular attack. The Reformers focused on the preaching and teaching of the Word of God as the unique way by which God's grace is apprehended. Though the recovery of the proclamation of the Good News is something to be celebrated, one also has to reflect on what might have been lost. Even Protestant scholar James White has wondered why believers wouldn't want to *increase* the sacramentals, the places where God is remembered and honored, rather than *decrease* them — as both Catholics and Protestants did during the Reformation. Might not such objects and practices, rather than disrupting a genuine faith, nurture it?

Finally, consider the particular *space of worship,* considered sacred because of the relics and the host that were found there. Unlike the space of modern Catholic churches, broken up in multiple ways, the space of medieval churches was open and fluid. Since pews, smaller chapels, and side altars didn't appear until the fifteenth century, the wide open, soaring space of medieval churches would have served to draw worshipers forward, and to direct their eyes to the vaulted ceilings above — frequently decorated by mosaics or frescoes of sacred events. There in the center, at the point at which the nave met the transepts, the altar was placed, often slightly raised above the level of the nave. Both its prominence and its centrality spoke to worshipers of the central sacrifice of Christ, remembered (and represented) in the events of the mass.

The space, objects, and actions of the medieval church all focused on the performance of the mass. And the events of this ancient liturgy in turn centered on the central event of the consecration of the host. Much medieval (and, later, Reformation) debate centered on the precise meaning both of Christ's words of institution — "This is my body" — and of the moment of transubstantiation — when the priest raised the host and the bell was rung, signaling the moment when the wafer became Christ's actual body. The medieval discussion focused primarily on the relationship between the substance and the acci-

Figure 1. Interior of nave of medieval cathedral in Reims, France.

dents of the host. That is, while the host retained the "accidents" or outward characteristics of a physical wafer, its "substance" or inner reality was changed into the actual body of Christ during the mass. While the Reformers later re-interpreted the "real presence" in ways consistent with their theology, its importance to medieval worshipers cannot be overstated. For them the real presence was less a theological truth than a religious reality. Christ's presence in the mass answered a fundamental question: In the midst of life's difficulties and in view of one's mortality, where can the comfort and presence of God be found? And if God is present in the event of the mass, as the church taught, the host is the place where this presence can be seen, touched, and even tasted. Participation in the Eucharist, usually only in one kind — of the wafer — was for medieval believers the privileged site of the divine presence. They believed that those who denied this "presence" — represented, for example, by the Cathars, who rejected Christ's physical resurrection and thus his physical presence in the host — were surely heretics who endangered not only people's faith but their very understanding of communal life.

The Elements of the Medieval Mass

Whatever disagreements Christians have over the precise form of this presence, the fact of God's presence in worship is the universal premise of worship — all Christian worship is predicated on a "real presence" of Christ, however this is understood. This will be the major feature of our discussion in the next chapter. Arguably, the debates over the form this takes all derive, in one way or another, from the medieval discussions about the presence of Christ. But beyond these discussions, the liturgical shape of this presence — the medieval mass, itself the product of centuries of conversation and controversy — lies behind all subsequent Christian worship. Even for those who call themselves nonliturgical, the medieval shape of the Ordinary of the Mass — that is, the "ordinary" structure of the mass unaltered by special liturgical celebrations like Christmas or Easter — is surely foundational for all subsequent developments in worship, whether churches followed this order closely or at a distance.

While there was some variation in the performance of the mass, six elements were considered essential. We will survey them briefly as the Kyrie, the Gloria, the Credo, the Sanctus, and the Agnus Dei, and we will add the Benediction, the final blessing.

Critical to every celebration of the mass was the singing or saying, usually at or near the beginning of the mass, of the *Kyrie Eleison:* "Lord, have mercy upon us." Here the priest led the congregation in corporate recognition of their inability to come into God's presence on the strengths of their own merits. The ancient awareness of Christians, schooled in Scripture and troubled by their own failings, comes to expression in this central prayer for God's mercy, and as this was elaborated in the medieval understanding of penance. While confession and forgiveness — or penance, as it was called — was a separate sacrament in the medieval period, its essential nature was acknowledged at the beginning of the mass. In subsequent mainline Protestant worship, this often takes the form of specific prayers of confession and requests for God's mercy and forgiveness. In Orthodox worship it is implicit in this oft-repeated prayer: "Lord, have mercy; Christ, have mercy; Lord, have mercy."

Next came the *Gloria Patri,* the expression of praise to God's glory as it endures through all time and beyond. From the time of the ancient Psalms of David, praise has been considered the centerpiece of Christian worship, its significance indicated in the famous declaration that God actually inhabits the praise of his people: "Yet you are holy, enthroned on the praises of Israel" (Ps. 22:3). Notice that these two elements — Kyrie and Gloria — take the form of prayer, so that in a sense it is redundant to say that worship includes prayer. Worship focuses on prayer to such an extent that, in the Orthodox tradition, for example, notions of worship and of prayer are virtually interchangeable.

But in the medieval mass, other elements besides prayer were also included, as the *Credo* of the mass indicates. "Credo" represents the first and principal word of the creed: "I believe . . ." In developing medieval worship, this often took the form of an actual recitation of a creed, and this practice continues in many traditions to this day. But surely this affirmation includes the element of hearing Scripture read and expounded in the form of a sermon or homily, a practice that has existed in Christian worship from the time of the Acts of the Apostles. This was certainly prominent in medieval worship as well, encouraged by the arrival of Mendicant orders of preachers — the Dominicans and the Franciscans — of the thirteenth century, who were highly trained in the art of preaching. After the Reformation, so-called noncreedal churches often renounced formal recitation of creeds in favor of the reading of and reflection on Scripture. But, whether formally or informally, worshipers in the Christian tradition all gather together, in part, to affirm their faith in God.

But I have argued that the logic of the mass during the Middle Ages moved toward the central moment of the consecration of the host in the Eucharist. This event was signaled by the element of medieval worship represented by the *Sanctus:* "Holy, holy, holy are you, O Lord." This too is a prayer and a pronouncement of the holiness of God and the reality of the divine presence in worship. Usually this immediately follows the words of institution and is often accompanied by the "fraction" or the breaking of the bread, signifying the body of Christ broken for us. In modern worship this holiness may be represented in the communion prayer or hymn. In whatever form or wherever it is found in the service, the acknowledgment of God's holiness is a central element of Christian worship.

Then comes the *Agnus Dei:* "Behold the Lamb of God, who takes away the sins of the world." To medieval worshipers, this was the moment when the sacrifice of Christ was (re)presented before them. Whether in the form of Eucharist (i.e., thanksgiving) or communion, all Christian churches celebrate this event by recalling the night on which the Lord was betrayed and took bread, blessed it, and broke it. For those in the Catholic and the Orthodox traditions, this constitutes the center of the worship service, while in most Protestant services, the Credo and the sermon are more likely to be the focus of worship.

Concluding the service was the *Benediction,* when the priest pronounced the blessing of the God who had been physically present in the sacrificial offering of Christ's body. In the well-known closing words, the priest said, *"Ite, missa est"* — "Go, it is sent" (from which the term *mass* was derived). The blessing implies the continuing presence of God as worshipers leave the sacred space of the church and go out (are sent) into what medieval believers saw as the secular places of the world.

These six elements constitute the structure of medieval worship. While there are, subsequently, wide varieties in the expression of these ancient elements, it is clear that the basic movement of this liturgy must be seen as central to the course of Christian worship.

Medieval Efforts to Stimulate Deeper Faith — and Their Abuse

A persistent concern of the many medieval reformers was capturing the attention (and deepening the understanding) of the crowds of medieval worshipers. Undoubtedly when Pope Urban II granted a plenary indulgence for participation in the First Crusade in 1096, he felt, rightly or wrongly, that he was encouraging a deeper participation of these pilgrims in the liturgical drama of the Christian life. Based on Matthew 18:18 and the power of the keys given to Peter, an indulgence was the church's remission of the temporal penalty for sin that had been confessed and forgiven, which resulted in a reduction of the time spent in purgatory. Though indulgences were later subject to much abuse, like the penitential system to which they were related, they were intended to encourage a deeper seriousness on the part of believers toward the church's teaching and their own moral lives. The preaching of the Mendicant orders and the practices they encouraged were similarly intended to promote a renewal of these ancient worship practices. In light of our contemporary concern for the renewal of worship, a brief sampling of these forms of renewal is instructive.

Of the many traditions instituted during the Late Middle Ages to stimulate lagging faith, two are worthy of mention here: the mystery plays and the attempts to stimulate an emotional identification with Christ's sufferings represented by the portrayal of the Pietà. We noted earlier that these and other efforts at reform owed a great deal to the

Figure 2. La Compagnia de' Colombari in *Laude in Urbis,* an ancient mystery play performed in 2005 in Orvieto, Italy, under the direction of Karin Coonrod.

rise in the early thirteenth century of the Mendicant orders, founded by Saint Dominic and Saint Francis. Usually more highly educated than parish priests, these friars went out to the towns and the countryside to preach against heresy and to encourage the faith of the people and a concern for the poor. Saint Francis in particular did more than any other figure of the Early Renaissance to stimulate the imagination of people to experience more deeply the stories of the Gospel. During one preaching mission he famously had the people act out the events of the Nativity to deepen their appreciation for Christ's humble birth. This impulse stimulated the rise of the mystery plays, which developed in thirteenth-century England and Italy. During special feast days, troupes of performers would enact the events of the history of salvation, especially those of the life of Christ, including his death and descent into hell. The events were acted out at various points in the city, and large crowds of people would follow the players through the narrow streets. In this way they were enabled to literally follow Christ as he went down through the jaws of death into hell, an experience that graphically reminded them that they would not escape this fate except through the means of salvation offered by the church.

The mystery plays and the concern of Saint Francis in particular were directed toward encouraging a closer connection with the life of Christ. Such efforts were given impetus by the grim progress of the Plague beginning in the second half of the fourteenth century. In some cities, up to a third of the population died during these outbreaks. These awful attacks motivated some to live only for the day, but stimulated others to reflect more deeply on their eternal destiny. Partly as a result of this, and the Franciscan focus on feeling more generally, there arose in the fifteenth century efforts to kindle an emotional identification with the sufferings of Christ. Nourished by the cult venerating the Virgin Mary, which had received fresh impetus during the twelfth century, artists began, first in Germany and then in Italy, to portray the Virgin holding her dead child on her lap after he had been taken down from the cross. These images came to be called "pietàs." Appearing twenty-three times in the Latin Vulgate, the word *pietas* could mean "mercy" (as in the mercy of God) or "religion" (or "charitable gift"), but in the medieval period it came to speak of the growing internalization of faith. It is interesting that this word, which would be so central to John Calvin's theology, would be identified here with the emotional suffering of Mary for her son, visually portrayed so as to arouse the faith and gratitude of viewers for the sufferings of Christ on their behalf.

Note how the two developments described here — the mystery plays and the Pietà motif — underline the connection between worship practices and the work of artists during this period. Plays, musical settings for the mass, altarpieces, and, later, smaller devotional artworks — all were integrated into the worship life of the people, and it is impossible to imagine medieval worship apart from these artistic forms. Indeed, it is impossible to understand the subsequent development of these art forms apart from this period. But just as art could be used to stimulate devotion, it could also reflect the abuse to which

Figure 3. Michelangelo's *Pietà*, St. Peter's Basilica, Vatican State.

this devotion was subject. By the mid-fourteenth century, artists began to find patrons among the emerging elite who were beneficiaries of the economic prosperity that followed in the aftermath of the Plagues and from the rise of cities. These wealthy patrons often turned to artists to publicize not only their success but also their piety.

30

Perhaps inevitably, art came to be tainted by the abuse of indulgences, as wealthy patrons eagerly endowed chapels and altarpieces in exchange for special masses and prayers for themselves and their families "in perpetuity."

One representative example of this trend is Jan van Eyck's *The Madonna of Chancellor Rolin,* painted about 1435. The presence of the donor kneeling before Mary, in what is surely meant to be an image of heaven, indicates the impact that private patronage was having on the use of images in worship — perhaps even on the nature of medieval worship itself. Here the worshiper, by virtue of his office and wealth (Rolin was one of the wealthiest men of Bruges, Belgium, owning many of the buildings visible in the background of van Eyck's painting, from which he extracted outrageous rents), intrudes into this sacred space, previously reserved for the Holy Family and various saints. This is perhaps the first time a donor appears in such a space without the sponsorship of a saint.

It was well-known that as a prominent member of the Court of Philip the Good, Rolin was as powerful as he was unscrupulous. That Rolin intended this commission to be an act of penance is clear from the fact that there was previously a large purse hanging from his side (subsequently painted over). In the garden outside the throne room of the Virgin, van Eyck has placed peacocks, symbolic of worldly pride, raising the question of whether this act of penance is really sincere. In this image van Eyck manages to capture the ambiguity not only of this act of penance but of the entire penitential system itself. The image illustrates and embodies historian Steven Ozment's observation about this period: "The road to the Reformation was paved by both unprecedented abuse and a long-unsatisfied religious longing."[4]

The Reformation cannot be understood apart from the abuse of religious objects and images, of course. But the focus on abuse, important as this is for what follows, leaves out a critical factor that

4. Steven Ozment, *The Age of Reform, 1250-1550: An Intellectual and Religious History of Late Medieval and Reformation Europe* (New Haven: Yale University Press, 1980), p. 211.

Figure 4. Jan van Eyck, *The Madonna of Chancellor Rolin,* The Louvre, Paris.

Carlos Eire has called "the metaphysics of worship" — that is, the positive role that symbolic acts, objects, and spaces continued to play throughout this period.[5] Many in the church knew that a reform of the abuses was increasingly necessary. The question facing the reformers of worship was whether the abuses could be addressed without de-

5. Carlos Eire frequently makes this point in *War Against the Idols.*

stroying the practices that nourished the worshiping life of medieval believers. Does reform necessarily mean the abolition of the practices? With this question in mind — a question that scholars debate to this day — we turn to two major figures of the Reformation.

The Reformation and the Quest for a Purified Worship

Martin Luther

In 1516, when Martin Luther nailed his famous theses on the church door in Wittenberg as a challenge to debate, he focused most of his attention on the abuses of worship, and on indulgences in particular. His own experience of God's grace had led him to oppose seeing these practices as vehicles of God's mercy rather than simply a means of spiritual discipline. Such things had become, in Luther's mind, a stairway that humans sought to build up to God, practices that obstructed the truth of the Gospel: that God has come down to us in Christ. Luther's great discovery was that we are justified not by our performance of religious ceremonies but by our faith in Christ's work.

Luther's joyful discovery of God's grace freely given in Christ followed from his reading and teaching of Scripture. First he discovered in the Psalms the greatness of the "righteousness of God," which the psalmist describes as "the mighty mountains" (Ps. 36:6). When he came to lecture on Paul's letter to the Romans, Luther realized that this righteousness was available to the believer by a heartfelt trust alone (Rom. 1:17). This led him to reject totally the medieval attempt to give some shape to God and thus corrupt worship. This is what he wrote about such practices in his lectures on the first chapter of Romans:

> Their error was that in their worship they did not take the Godhead for what it is in itself, but changed it by fitting it to their own needs and desires. Everyone wanted the Godhead to be in him whom he happened to like, and thus they turned the truth of God into a lie. . . . So they worship the product of their own imagination more

33

truly than the true God himself, who they believe resembles this product of their fancy.[6]

God had come to us in Christ. This Gospel story is found in what Luther called the "manger" of God's Word. To find the mercy of God, we come, like the Wise Men, to the manger. For Luther, then, idolatry was a matter of the heart. Once the heart was cleansed of the human tendency toward self-justification, what one did about external matters in worship was not important.

Clearly, Luther's great rediscovery that the just "will live by faith" was a momentous event that has affected all subsequent discussions of faith and worship. But his unblinking focus on faith led him to sidestep the substantial nature of worship and the possible forms it should take. He felt comfortable, for the most part, in continuing the medieval structure of the mass.

Not all those working with Luther agreed with his tolerance with respect to medieval practices. His colleague Andreas Karlstadt took the opportunity of Luther's absence in 1522 to instigate acts of iconoclasm, destroying images and objects important to medieval worship. When Luther returned, he upbraided Karlstadt. During an important series of Easter sermons in 1523, Luther insisted that these outward things are not the important concern. It is the Word of God faithfully preached that causes the abuses to cease. Luther claimed to have done nothing himself to bring down the papacy; the Word that Luther preached had done this of its own accord. Thus, Luther continued, if it were preached that "images were nothing and that no service is done to God by erecting them; then they would have fallen of themselves."[7] Images and sacramentals could be used in teaching, Luther believed, but they provided nothing essential.

But are images really "nothing," as Luther taught? If they are, how does one account for the power of the sacraments? If such symbolic

6. Luther, *Lectures on Romans,* trans. Wilhelm Pauck (Philadelphia: Westminster Press, 1961), pp. 23-24, 26.

7. *Selected Writings of Martin Luther,* ed. Theodore Tappert (Philadelphia: Fortress Press, 1967), vol. 2, p. 247.

entities do no service to God, what do we make of the Eucharist? Luther himself surely did not mean that images are nothing, for he had a relatively high view of the Lord's Supper, believing that Christ's presence was in, with, and under the substance of the meal. And he was inclined to include acts of penance as a third sacrament, alongside baptism and the Lord's Supper. So, while he recovered the centrality of preaching the Good News, he did not help to develop the worship practices that best expressed and celebrated this liberating reality.

John Calvin

John Calvin had more definite — and more clearly negative — ideas about medieval practices. When he arrived in Geneva in 1536, the city fathers had already sided with the reform that Luther had set loose. The city council had already voted to abolish the medieval mass in Geneva. Yet Calvin later confessed that there really had been no reformation at all when he arrived. What, then, did he believe real reform would look like?

We get some idea of his notion of reform from the two major efforts to which he turned his attention after his arrival in Geneva. First, he began to issue regular editions of his teaching about the Christian life, what he called the *Institutes.* There, roughly following the Apostles' Creed, he offers an outline of the Christian life. For Calvin, the "faith" that Luther discovered must be elaborated in an ordered instruction that could structure believers' lives. There is evidence, in fact, that Calvin imagined that he was producing a kind of Protestant verbal icon by which believers were to arrange their lives and deepen their faith. Through regular instruction and the resulting reflection, believers would be shaped into the likeness of Christ.

Second, Calvin, like Luther before him, turned his attention early on to teaching children, issuing his first catechism in 1541.[8] Each

8. See John Calvin, *Theological Treatises,* edited and translated with notes by J. K. S. Reid (Philadelphia: Westminster Press, 1954), pp. 91-139.

Sunday children were required to come for instruction on the questions that made up the catechism. Notice carefully what Calvin was doing: He was replacing the external visual images and practices that structured the lives of medieval believers with a systematic teaching of God's Word for both children and adults. Within barely a generation, the symbolic images and actions were entirely eliminated in favor of Calvin's careful program of instruction and regular preaching of Scripture. The practices of worship came to center on the preaching of the Word, which, with the attendant instruction, was to represent a performance that was to shape the whole of believers' lives in the world. All of this was meant to reflect what Calvin understood by "piety" (or *pietas*), the sense of living all of life in the presence of a loving and holy God. He describes piety as "that reverence joined with love of God which the knowledge of his benefits induces." It exists when believers "recognize that they owe everything to God, that they are nourished by his fatherly care, that he is the Author of their every good."[9] Until they realize this, Calvin says, believers will never yield themselves fully in service to God.

What is the nature of true worship for Calvin that comports best with this piety? In the catechism he outlines four elements. First, we are to put our whole trust in God. This is represented, in Calvin's mind, by the regular reciting of the Apostles' Creed, which became a regular part of worship in Geneva (and, indeed, in much subsequent Protestantism). Second, we are called to serve him with our whole life. Here Calvin continues the New Testament conflation of service and worship (for which the same word is often used; see Rom. 12:1-2). This aspect is represented in worship by the reading of the Law from both the Old and the New Testaments, and the subsequent exposition of Scripture in the sermon. Third, we are to take refuge in God at all times. This aspect is seen in the central role of prayer in worship, and in the Lord's Prayer in particular, which was regularly recited in

9. John Calvin, *Institutes of the Christian Religion,* trans. Ford Lewis Battles, ed. John T. McNeill (Philadelphia: Westminster Press, 1960), 1.2.1. Subsequent references to this work will be made parenthetically in the text.

Genevan worship. Finally, we are to respond to God in faith and thus be united to him. Calvin believes that this is best imaged in the Eucharist, which pictures this spiritual uniting of the believer with Christ.

Thus Calvin retained most of the elements of medieval worship. Services in Geneva included prayer, the recitation of the creed, the reading of Scripture and preaching, and, finally, the Eucharist (which Calvin unsuccessfully sought to celebrate weekly). Indeed, the movement of the service would continue to echo the medieval mass. But the elements now were placed in a highly developed theological framework in which the relationship between these practices and believers' lives in the world was carefully explained.

Sacraments, which for Calvin included baptism and the Lord's Supper, were signs that "show forth" the nature of the Gospel. As elsewhere, here there is a clear pedagogical intent in Calvin's understanding. Calvin often used the image of God's condescension to humanity, of God's babbling to them as a nursemaid would to a baby, thus using an image that they could understand. Calvin believed that the Eucharist as "image" leads believers by the hand to show forth Christ, "and show him forth to be known" (4.14.20). Christ is ascended to the right hand of God, Calvin taught, but the Spirit lifts believers through the sacrament and spiritually joins them with Christ in the heavenly places.

Here the sacrament is a very particular (and for Calvin very important) instance of the more general way that God works in worship. In his instruction for preachers in the catechism, for example, Calvin taught,

> In the preaching of the word, the external minister holds forth the vocal word, and it is received by the ears. The internal minister the Holy Spirit truly communicates the thing proclaimed through the word that is Christ to the souls of all who will, so that it is not necessary that Christ or for that matter his word be received through the organs of the body, but the Holy Spirit effects this union by his secret virtue, by creating faith in us by which he makes us living members of Christ.[10]

10. Calvin, *Theological Treatises*, p. 173.

37

It is clear that Calvin believed that preaching of this kind should supplant all the many ways in which medieval believers sought to come to God. "In the preaching of his Word and sacred mysteries," Calvin taught, "[God] has bidden that a common doctrine be there set forth for all. But those whose eyes rove about in contemplating idols betray that their minds are not diligently set upon this doctrine" (1.11.7). The reason for this replacement is both positive and negative. This medium of preaching represents the better way that God can be apprehended, but it also supplants those other forms which, for Calvin, clearly cannot hold God. We should not dare to subject God, "who is incomprehensible, to our sense perceptions or to represent him by any form" (2.8.17).

For Calvin, preaching replaced these other media, especially in its ability to image biblical truth. In true preaching, "'Christ is depicted before our eyes as crucified' [Gal. 3:1]. . . . From this one fact they could have learned more than from a thousand crosses of wood or stone" (1.11.7). So, in preaching, believers are enabled by the internal ministry of the Holy Spirit to "see" what was previously invisible, and to understand what was formerly incomprehensible to them, even if the seeing is done primarily with their minds and hearts. In the medieval period, the image of Christ on the cross dominated virtually every worship space; the Reformers who followed Calvin sought to banish even an empty cross. Negatively, the reasons for this lay in the superstition to which such images had been subject. But positively, Calvin believed that if Christ is truly preached, all such images are unnecessary. Ironically, Calvin placed a very high value on verbal images that "pictured" for the imagination the heart of Jesus or the role of the cross — he could actually use the word *painting* for such portrayals. But actual visual images could play no role in his spirituality.

In Book Two of Calvin's *Institutes* there is only a simple, one-page description of the actual event of the cross (2.16.6). But elsewhere in the *Institutes* Calvin will expound at great length on the *importance* of the cross in our lives (see 3.8): We "pass our lives under a continual cross"; as Christ suffered, we will expect that we too will suffer; and so on. This all develops Calvin's unique understanding of *pietas* as living the whole of life in the presence of God. The medieval notion of *pietas* as a developing emotional identification with Christ's suffering has been completely reconfigured. The actual image of a dead Christ in Mary's lap has become a theological image of each believer imagining life lived in a cross-shaped, self-sacrificing way. Ignatius Loyola, the famous Counter-Reformation saint, in continuity with the medieval notion of *pietas,* will urge believers in his *Spiritual Exercises* (c. 1526) to imagine every detail of the events of the life of Christ, so that believers might experience them *as if they themselves were present.* John Calvin, by contrast, will instruct believers to understand that their lives should take on the shape of the cross. In the one interpretation, transformation is understood as following upon absorption into the event of Christ's death; in the other, transformation is the result of believers' appropriating the theological meaning of that event in their lives.

Sometimes Calvin's teaching about worship is presented as overly cognitive and abstract, but he himself would have resisted this. Like Luther, Calvin encouraged animated congregational singing of the Psalms, which he felt engaged the heart of the worshiper. Moreover, he understood worship to be an experience of the whole person. He often spoke about the life of faith and of worship in dramatic terms. We are called to be players, he said, in the great theatre of God's redemption. Creation is the larger stage on which God's performance is played out. So, Calvin would say, the worship service is a local performance of this larger dramatic presentation. All of this comes to focus on the sermon and the Eucharist as a kind of play within a play, drawing worshipers into the dramatic actions of God in the world.[11]

In an interesting footnote to his instructions on church order, Calvin insists that outside of the hours of service, the church building is to be locked. This was to be done so that "no one outside the hours may enter for superstitious reasons. If anyone be found making any particular devotion inside or nearby, he is to be admonished; if it ap-

11. This idea is developed in Michael Horton, *Covenant and Eschatology: The Divine Drama* (Louisville: Westminster John Knox, 2002). See Chapter Nine, "Community Theatre," pp. 265-76.

pears to be a superstition which he will not amend, he is to be chastised."[12] Going regularly into the church to pray before an image, to light candles, or to sit quietly and reflect is henceforth forbidden. Now prayer and reflection have no special connection with this space, with any object found therein, or with any particular action that might be observed there. Here we might wonder what might have been lost from Calvin's locked — and increasingly barren — church space. What was for medieval worshipers something to be seen came to be understood in the Reformation as something to be heard — the ear came to be privileged over the eye. Clearly, Calvin's emphasis on preaching and teaching, even the dramatic involvement of worshipers in Christ's cross-shaped life, did much to renew worship for many. But, at the same time, did the elimination of devotional objects and actions reduce the places for the emotional connection with the experience of worship?

Conclusion

Faithful medieval worshipers — and, indeed, Catholic believers of the Counter-Reformation — might have lamented all that was lost by the process of reform. Now God was met specially in the preaching of the Word and the instructions of Scripture, but outside of the preaching and the Eucharist, there was no particular place, no special object or activity, by which this might be enriched or set forth. There was nothing to touch, see, or experience that would set forth the palpable connection with this faith. Unlike the medieval worship space, the "new" worship space had no place where believers could stand to see images, no details of architecture, no ceremony or enactment that would speak about their faith.

But one must also celebrate all that was gained in the Reformation. The prayers, the preaching, the congregational singing of Calvin's church in Geneva — surely these were transformative (and emo-

12. Calvin, *Theological Treatises*, p. 79.

tional) experiences for many. Additionally, prayer, worship, and devotion were now understood to relate to the whole of life. Beauty and goodness were not the special province of church buildings and their furnishings, but were to be seen, potentially at least, at every point in God's good creation and in human vocation. In Calvin's arresting image, creation is now seen as a "theatre" for the glory of God. *Pietas* has been reframed. Rather than seeing suffering supremely in the agony of Christ, as the Dutch theologian Abraham Kuyper put it, believers are to see a mystical suffering in the general woe of humankind.[13]

There is, further, a clear ethical renewal that is implied in all of this. The true image and presence of God is not to be identified with physical images but is to be sought in our neighbor, according to the Reformers. Calvin insists that we not look at the evil in our neighbors, "but . . . look upon the image of God in them . . . , with its beauty and dignity [which] allures us to love and embrace them" (3.7.6). As a result, the Reformers would make this plea: Do not spend precious resources on erecting images of saints and holy personages. Use these resources to feed and clothe your neighbor, to love and embrace the flesh-and-blood images of God.

Both Luther and Calvin have dramatically reframed the setting of worship. The performance of preaching, the recitation of the creed, and the celebration of the Eucharist point us to the dramatic reversal that is represented by the death and resurrection of Christ. In turn we are to re-enact this drama as we seek to reconstruct the world after the fashion of the new creation inaugurated by Christ's death and resurrection. In Calvin's day the need for this re-ordering was critical, because half the population of Geneva was desperately poor. The death of Christ, then, is not an event intended to make us cry, or to squirm in our seats, as suggested by Mel Gibson's *The Passion of the Christ.* Rather, it is an event that is to transform us into agents of the new order there initiated.

13. Abraham Kuyper, *Lectures on Calvinism* (Grand Rapids: William B. Eerdmans, 1931 [1898]), pp. 166, 167.

The content of this new teaching is clear enough, especially to most Protestants. But the question of the appropriate form of this content continues to bedevil discussions of worship, as we will see. What forms of worship constitute fitting carriers of the biblical Good News that the Reformers celebrated?

These two streams — medieval worship and Reformation spirituality — have continued to determine the development of Christian worship in both its Catholic and its Protestant forms. James White emphasizes the split between the two churches that the Reformation caused: "A common heritage became two completely separate histories of development in mutual indifference."[14] For better or worse, this common influence was splintered into the multiple forms that Christianity has taken since that period, which we will review in the next chapter. It is true that in the last half of the twentieth century, there has been a convergence, or at least a mutual influence, between and among the forms of Christian worship. However, the resulting tensions, conversations, and reactions all reflect in one way or another the issues that we have surveyed in this chapter. Indeed, I will argue that for all the declarations of advance and creativity in contemporary worship, the controversies that swirl around it are anything but new. And they call us all to reflect on the sources of our inclinations, and even our prejudices, as we seek to be faithful worshipers in the twenty-first century.

SUGGESTIONS FOR FURTHER READING

William Dyrness. *Reformed Theology and Visual Culture: The Protestant Imagination from Calvin to Edwards.* Cambridge: Cambridge University Press, 2004.

Carlos M. N. Eire. *War Against the Idols.* Cambridge: Cambridge University Press, 1986.

14. James F. White, *Protestant Worship: Traditions in Transition* (Louisville: Westminster John Knox, 1989), p. 28.

J. A. Jungmann. *Mass of the Roman Rite.* London, 1959.

Edward Muir. *Ritual in Early Modern Europe.* Cambridge: Cambridge University Press, 2005.

Calvin Stapert. *A New Song for an Old World: Musical Thought in the Early Church.* Grand Rapids: William B. Eerdmans, 2007.

James White. *The Sacraments in Protestant Practice and Faith.* Nashville: Abingdon Press, 1999.

QUESTIONS FOR DISCUSSION

1. Think of your worship tradition. What is emphasized in the worship service? What are the strengths and weaknesses of this emphasis? Where do you think this emphasis came from?

2. Discuss the notion of "sacred space." What is it, or what should it be? In your mind, is it a positive notion (does it provide a means of growing closer to God) or a negative one (does it erect a barrier to our growth in Christ)?

3. The so-called Emergent Church (the twenty-something worship in North America, Britain, and Australia) is seeking to recover medieval practices in their worship. Do you think this is a good thing or a bad thing? Why?

4. "In many ways the Reformation was disastrous to a fully-orbed understanding of worship in its historical and cultural settings." Discuss this proposition. In what ways is it true? In what ways false?

5. Do you think that true worship requires some physical or material "carrier" to be effective? Why or why not?

CHAPTER 3

From Then Till Now

*How Styles of Spirituality Shape
Current Christian Worship*

What, Then, Is Worship?

In the last chapter we reviewed briefly the medieval background of
worship and the renewal represented by the Reformation. A fuller
treatment would have included more of the reform from the Catholic
side in what was called the Counter-Reformation. But my argument is
that both the medieval tradition, which continues in the Catholic tradition, and the spirituality that developed during the Protestant Reformation continue to nurture Christian worship in all the various
forms it has subsequently taken. At the same time, the issues raised
during the Reformation over the form of worship have continued rele-
vance for our contemporary discussions — especially the replacing of
external forms with an internal focus. In this chapter I will review a
sampling of forms that developed in the Protestant world and describe some of the ferment these developments led to in the twentieth
century.

If it is true that by the Reformation all the elements were in place,
deriving from Scripture and the traditions drawing on them, to define
the essentials of Christian worship, we should now be in a position to
sketch out, in a preliminary way, these essentials. Let me offer here an
initial definition of worship with which we will work in the following

44

chapters. I present this in the form of a confession, to underline its communal character and its role as an aspect of our public faith:

> Christians believe that worship is (1) a set of culturally embedded and corporate practices (2) through which God forms them into the likeness of Christ, (3) in and through the story of Jesus Christ, (4) by the power of the Holy Spirit, in order that (5) they might live their lives to the glory of God.

Let us look briefly at these five elements. First of all, worship is, above all, *a communal set of practices* — that is, worship is something that Christians as the people of God do together. Even though they also do some of these things in their private or family devotions — pray, offer praise, or whatever — Christians believe that they join with other Christians in all places and, in the case of praise, even with the hosts of heaven when they engage in corporate worship. But, at the same time, it is important to stress that these practices are, inevitably, culturally embedded. That is, they will always reflect the particular cultural (and historical) setting in which they develop: African worship reflects the lively character of its corporate life; Anglican worship reflects its British setting; Latin-American Pentecostalism takes on a Latin temperament; and so on. Worship is a particular kind of cultural space, as I emphasized in the introduction; the practices of worship kindle a specific set of expectations that set it apart from the culture around it. Nevertheless, the practices of worship will surely, for better or worse, reflect on and engage the wider culture. We will consider in detail the problems and the opportunities this offers as we go along.

While the practices involved are not *limited* to particular times when God's people gather together, they especially *characterize* these special times — and this corporate celebration will be the major emphasis of our reflections. Further, as I emphasized in the introduction, these are theological practices. That is, the practices of worship are theologically informed. They are what philosophers call "theory laden": they depend on and embody a set of beliefs about God. Worship reflects and responds to particular ways that God has promised to be present and to bless believers. Christians in fact believe that God is involved in a direct way in these events. The objects and actions of worship are transparent to the divine presence.

A focus on practices carries a particular liability that needs to be acknowledged. Since they are actions of imperfect people, one cannot simply claim that worship practices are *automatically* theological events. Indeed, worship practices can be poorly or thoughtlessly performed — they can be done, as Catholics say, without "proper intention." Moreover, the repeated performance of even noble activities does not necessarily make people better. Anyone who has ever attended a church for any length of time can attest to these limitations. At the same time, the actions we speak of share historical and biblical precedents that constitute them as human responses to God's initiative. Declaring them theological practices, then, is an expression of our biblical faith in God. Steadfastly following this pattern expresses the faith of God's people that though we perform this "work," the effects will be the gifts of God's grace. As Paul says, "Work out your own salvation . . . ; for it is God who is at work in you" (Phil. 2:12-13). To insist that we should avoid specific practices of worship because they can be abused is to doubt what God has promised.[1]

Because of these dangers, there have been those, especially in the Protestant tradition, who have questioned this emphasis on practices. Since the Reformation, some Protestant denominations and theological traditions, especially various Pietist and Quaker groups, have focused their attention on the inward aspect of faith. These would affirm the corporate dimension but would place more emphasis on the inclination of the heart than on outward actions. But as we saw in the last chapter, even during the Reformation, the major Reformers instituted forms and practices — catechisms, singing, creeds, and so on — that they felt better reflected (and communi-

---

1. See the excellent discussion of this issue in Simon Chan, *Liturgical Theology: The Church as Worshiping Community* (Downers Grove, Ill.: InterVarsity Press, 2007), Chapter Four.

cated) the truth of the Gospel and of Scripture. All the while, of course, they were aware of the danger of forms that could lose their meaning. In a sense, one might say that an emphasis on "practice" was challenged by the inward turn of the Reformation, but in the end this was reframed rather than abolished. While formalism was resisted, the use of forms persisted.

Thus I will argue that worship always involves people doing things — recall that liturgy is "the work of the people." A wide variety of liturgical actions have been developed by Christians, in addition to the major sacraments, as they have sought to be true to Scripture and their faith — from foot-washing to infant dedication. But in every case, Christian worship involves the regular performance of specified actions as the necessary medium of both spiritual blessing and human obedience. These are necessary because they facilitate that two-directional movement that I have stressed — the movement of God to the people and that of the people back to God.

Second, people perform the practices of worship in the belief that *by these actions God will form them into the likeness of Christ.* It has been the conviction of believers since biblical times that doing certain things together is spiritually transformative. This was true of the Old Testament sacrifices and the pilgrimages to Jerusalem. It was also evident when, in the New Testament, believers in Acts gathered together around the apostles' teaching, shared their goods, and met together to break bread and praise God. And in one form or another, Christians have joined in certain practices ever since. Being a Christian does not simply mean accepting certain truths, or even being a "moral" person, though it also means these things. Nor does it mean that these actions have intrinsic value in and of themselves, outside of the context of faith and obedience. Hypocrisy is a constant temptation in worship, as it is in all aspects of discipleship. But it is the Christian conviction that, in some central way, being a Christian means that certain practices — such as prayer, Scripture-reading, praise, and baptism — are essential markers of God's presence and our faithful human response (though, as we will discuss in Chapter Five, some practices carry more theological significance than others).

Notice that these practices have come to vary widely — a variation that we reflect on in this chapter. But there have always been scriptural or traditional limits to this variation. At the same time, as we have seen in the previous chapter, these practices, whatever scriptural warrant believers have claimed for them, inevitably have borne the mark of their historical, cultural, and theological contexts.

One of the boundaries that Christians of all kinds have placed on worship practice reflects the particular narrative to which this is connected. Christians believe that the practices of worship are to shape the believer *in and through the story of Jesus Christ.* Of course, all Christians also believe that the narrative of this life is vitally connected to God's creation of the world, the call of Israel, and the emerging of the young church in the New Testament, but it centrally focuses on the life, death, resurrection, and ascension of Jesus Christ. All Christians believe that this story is more than a morality tale; it is a series of events that structures all of history, accomplishes salvation, and thus forms the believer's spiritual life. Theologians have expressed this truth in various ways: Through our baptism we are joined with Christ's death and resurrection; the Christian life by the power of the Spirit becomes an extension of redemptive history, as accomplished in Christ; Christian discipleship follows ("imitates") Christ's life; the Christian life is cross-shaped; and so on. But in every case the goal in some way reflects the Christian view that believers are to grow into the likeness of Christ or be united with him in such a way that they share his nature. Christ, in both his earthly and his glorified life, is a model and, more than this, a "pioneer" of the person the Christian wishes — whether now or in heaven — to become.

The fourth element of this definition expresses a vital theological truth that is critical to the way Christians understand and engage in worship. The practices and the formation that result from worship are always dependent on the Holy Spirit. Worship, Christians believe, is *empowered by the Holy Spirit.* In other words, the performance of particular actions, the saying of certain words, even the focus of one's attention in special ways — these are not *in themselves* transformative. Now there are those who would argue that these practices may in fact

48

influence our consciousness in various ways — quieting us, perhaps slowing our heartbeat, and so on. But these physical changes are not what Christians mean by the transformation that worship brings about. The practices, though surely important, are merely carriers or instruments that allow God through the Holy Spirit to work in believers' lives. The exact relationship between the performance of certain practices and the action of the Spirit — who is authorized to say certain words or preside over services, which things are necessarily done and which might be optional — has been greatly contested in the history of Christian worship. But all would agree that in some way, true worship is dependent on the activity of the Holy Spirit.

Finally, Christian worship is directed toward a certain end: *that believers live their lives to the glory of God.* Though this may seem unproblematic, in fact it may be the most contested area of all. For there are Christians (certain Orthodox and Catholics, for example) who believe that the end of the practices of worship is largely internal. On this view, the goal of the Christian life *is* the practice of corporate worship, which is itself an anticipation of the worship of God in heaven. They would agree that worship certainly ought to influence the whole of life, but that goal would be subsidiary to the end of worship: standing in the presence of God. Here my definition reflects the Protestant (and Reformed) perspective that underlies this book. While believers in the Reformed tradition believe that worship — prayer, praise, testimony, and so on — is an end in itself, this end is part of a larger goal: that all of life, in whole and in part (including the part we call worship), should serve and reflect God's glory. Though Christians have appeared to differ on this issue, I would argue that, in the end, these views are not as far apart as they initially seem, or as our contentious history has sometimes made them appear. For it is not hard to see that worship and service are, in many ways, two sides of the same reality — as, indeed, all Christians would agree that they are. Standing in the presence of God and living out this presence in one's life are surely connected, and it is perhaps one of the sad lessons of our Christian history that we — Christians of all kinds — have not always understood and emphasized this properly.

Styles of Christian Worship in the Protestant Tradition

If there is such a fundamental agreement about the practices of worship, as I have argued, then this question arises: Why are there so many different and seemingly opposed ways in which these practices are shaped? There are many reasons for this. In large part, of course, the variations reflect the particular historical and cultural situations that shaped them, but I will be arguing that even widely differing activities can reflect (at least) overlapping spiritual commitments. Although proponents of certain traditions may argue for the uniqueness and purity of their "style" of worship, it is often (if not always) possible to see similarities and shared commitments in and through the differences. At least approaching things with this expectation might make it possible for adherents of one style to learn something worthy from the style of another.

I will be calling these differences "styles of spirituality," and it is important to understand what I mean by this way of putting things. While our focus is on worship, I prefer to use the term *spirituality* because these habits of religious practice, which we will examine, extend far beyond the corporate dimension of worship and, for many believers, shape the way they understand their lives as Christians. I believe that one's understanding of how life with God should be lived may be designated as one's spirituality. This includes simple practices — carrying cards of memory verses or a rosary, for example — that would not, strictly speaking, be a part of corporate worship.

A personal example may help explain what I have in mind. Though I didn't understand this until much later in life, I was raised in a tradition of spirituality that can be traced to the Lutheran Church in Norway and to the Pietist stream of that tradition in particular. This in turn was influenced by the Midwestern forms of Protestant fundamentalism and revivalism in which I was raised. These influences resulted in a particular mix of practices that shaped my early life as a Christian: praying before meals or when setting out on a trip; kneeling for a time of prayer after the evening meal; going to church twice on Sunday and to prayer meetings on Wednesday; giving my testimony before my baptism as an adult; and so on. Notice that these are all things that we *did* (though my parents would have been appalled to think that our spirituality depended on doing certain things — which they would have called "works righteousness"!). Notice further that these things represented a particular style of "spirituality" rather than of theology (to which they would be only indirectly related). I now know that this reflected a particular mix of Scandinavian Pietism and American revivalism, which emphasized a spirituality of crisis (the need for personal decision) and inward intensity (rather than outward emotional display). But at that time it was the only way that I knew how to be a Christian — indeed, I was fairly sure it was the *only* way of being a true Christian.

These reflections have led me to believe that we need to spend more time thinking about styles of spirituality — where their roots lie, and how they hold together and shape communities of faith. I use the term *style* to distinguish this from larger traditions of faith and theology. These habits of what might be called "popular faith" are in many ways more important to most believers than major traditions of theology, of which the average Christian may understand very little, and to which very little attention is paid. Of course, these popular forms could benefit from a deeper reflection on the theological issues that they express, and indeed, that is part of the reason for this book. Their differences often focus on language, but the issues involved are much deeper, reaching to practices and preferences that embody very different views of worship and formation. So we begin this descriptive survey of worship styles with the recognition that every person of faith inherits (or is converted into) a style of spirituality — which includes particular practices and various assumptions about faith and the presence of God.[2] Since many of these practices and assumptions are

2. The options of worship styles have been usefully surveyed in Lester Ruth, "A Rose by Any Other Name," in *The Conviction of Things Not Seen,* ed. Todd Johnson (Grand Rapids: Brazos Press, 2002). In what follows I have made use of his discussion, along with the descriptions of Jeanne Kilde in her book *When Church Became Theatre: The Transformation of Evangelical Architecture and Worship in Nineteenth-Century America* (Oxford: Oxford University Press, 2002), and those of James F. White

unexamined, it may be valuable to lay them out here for some preliminary inspection.

There is a further reason, at least for evangelical Protestants, for framing a discussion of worship in terms of spirituality. Growing up, I can hardly remember thinking of things I did as a Christian — such as praying and Bible-reading, even when I did them on Sunday — as "worship"; I certainly didn't think of them as "liturgy." But while I did not always connect these things with corporate worship, they had everything to do with my being truly "spiritual," which I would have said was the goal of my life. Words like *worship* and *liturgy* were simply not a part of my active Christian vocabulary — and, though this is changing, there are still many Christians who hesitate to use such words. "Liturgy" was what people did without thinking in churches that, as we believed, were dead or dying! It turns out, of course, that the things I did to be spiritual also had an influence on the particular order of things that happened on Sunday morning — the testimonies, the long, fervent prayers, and so on. And though we would not have called that "order of service" a liturgy, it did everything, even in overlapping ways, that a traditional liturgical service did. As we will see, these attitudes are changing in the new century. But old attitudes die hard, and framing a discussion of worship in terms of spirituality may make the conversation more accessible to some and will certainly be truer to the history and development of the styles we will briefly trace.

Since, in the last chapter, we left things at the period of the Reformation, it might be useful to pick up the story of developments in worship with the nearest heirs of the Calvinist Reformation: the Puritans.

Worship and Spirituality in Puritan New England

The worship of Puritan New England was the clearest incarnation of Reformation worship in the New World. It also embodies best what I

---

in *Protestant Worship: Traditions in Transition* (Louisville: Westminster John Knox, 1989). I have also benefited from conversations with Dr. Ed Phillips of Duke University, who is at work on a more substantial treatment of these matters.

am calling spirituality, for the theological practices encouraged during the seventeenth and eighteenth centuries were certainly not confined to the formal services on Sunday. Indeed, the space used for worship, called simply the "meetinghouse," pointedly did not carry any symbolic significance, outside of its location in or near the center of town (though one could argue that even this was a reality that was more pragmatic than symbolic — so everyone would be equally able to attend worship services and thus not run the risk of violating the Sabbath). The arrangement of pews around the simple communion table and the pulpit, which was sometimes the only object endowed with any special decoration, spoke of the simplicity of a worship focusing on the preaching and hearing of the Word of God.

Puritan spirituality reflected Calvin's emphasis on structuring all of life in a way that glorified God. This is true in two ways. First, for the most part, Puritans carefully followed Calvin's admonition that worship should be biblical (something that has come to be called "the regulative principle of worship"). That is, believers should follow patterns specified and modeled in Scripture and not add human practices that might run the risk of distorting biblical truth. Thus praying, singing, and reading and teaching Scripture were central to both domestic and corporate worship. But second, as this implies, these practices were in no way limited to the space or time of the church service. One of the reasons that Calvin locked the church building was surely to underline the point that one did not have to come to any special place to pray, but that all of life could become a sanctuary for believers' worship. So one was just as likely to hear Puritans singing hymns in the home, or even in the fields, as in the church service. Scripture reading and study were just as important during family time and personal quiet time as at church — indeed, the language of Scripture would have been a major influence on the development of the Puritans' broader culture. Prayer would have preceded any significant personal or social event, providing a spiritual structure for the life of the average Puritan.

These inclinations, however, led to a distinctive style of corporate worship that is important to describe. While the practices of worship would have been spread throughout the week, attendance at the weekly worship service (or services) was considered mandatory. As in the Middle Ages, the communal worship and the activities related to it were central to the cultural lives of the Puritans. The meetinghouse was the place they came for news, for social interaction, and for what we might call "entertainment" — indeed, for many it was the primary source of their formal education. Services might last as long as three hours, with the pastoral prayer sometimes extending over an hour, and sermons being of equal or greater length. Puritan sermons are famous, or notorious, depending on your perspective, for their dense theological content — in fact, some of Jonathan Edwards's most important theological work first saw the light of day in the form of sermons. Scholars estimate that Christians in this period would have heard more than five thousand sermons in their lifetime — probably equivalent to the number of films or videos that people see today over the course of their lives! We look back incredulously on such "entertainment," but there were actually times in New England when leaders had to restrict the number of sermons preached each week so that people would not neglect their work and families by running to and fro to hear the latest preacher. All variations of seasons — what we call the church year — and all ceremonies and pilgrimages were now eclipsed. In their place was the weekly worship service with its long sermons, prayers, and fervent singing.

What would the average worship service have looked like? It would have begun (and ended) with a blessing from the preacher, followed by the singing of a psalm. Consistent with the belief that worship was to be biblical, for the first hundred years or so after Calvin, singing would have been limited to singing the Psalms — which Puritans considered to be the Bible's hymnbook. The first book printed in America was the *Bay Psalm Book,* which translated the Psalms into language that could be sung — in church or at home. Gradually, hymns were introduced, though these were initially opposed as an unbiblical and overly emotional practice. By the early eighteenth century, respected (and biblical) hymn-writers like Isaac Watts made hymns a common part of worship.

The reading of Scripture appointed for the day would have followed the psalm or hymn, followed by another hymn or anthem. The sermon would come next, followed by what came to be called the pastoral prayer for and on behalf of the people. Unless communion was celebrated, which would have been done only monthly or quarterly, a final hymn would be followed by a blessing and the dismissal.

Clearly, there is continuity with Reformational worship, and indeed with elements of medieval worship as well. But equally interesting is the continuity with much Protestant worship today. The service as a whole was probably much more lively than we imagine it to be, since it was not uncommon for worship to include congregational discussion of the sermon or Scripture reading. In a place where everyone knew everyone else, the freedom to participate was probably greater than if fellow worshipers were strangers to each other — as is often the case today.

There were other Christian worship styles present in pre-Revolutionary America, such as those of the Quakers and, in the middle and southern states, the Anglicans, but the Puritan style of worship and spirituality was to leave its particular mark on American worship, especially in what we today call mainline churches. The relationship between this particular style and the styles that preceded and followed it is represented in Table 1 on page 56.

The Free Church Style: Worship and Spirituality in the Gathered Church

In a part of the Protestant Reformation that I have not yet described, reformers known as Anabaptists (so called because of their practice of baptizing adult "converts" who had previously been baptized as infants) radically transformed the accepted idea of the church. Since the time of Constantine in the fourth century A.D., it had been understood that every area would have one church (though divided into several congregations), to which everyone, at least nominally, would belong. Everyone born into this region (or parish) would have been baptized, or christened, in the church as an infant. There would have

Table 1. Continuities in American Mainline Worship

Ordinary of the Mass	New England Puritan Worship (Congregational), 1700-1800	Mainline Protestant Worship
Kyrie	Blessing	The Gathering: Call to worship/Confession
Gloria	Hymn	Hymn
Credo	Scripture	Creed/Scripture
	Sermon	Sermon
Sanctus	Prayer	Prayer
Agnus Dei	Eucharist (occasionally)	Eucharist
	Hymn	Hymn
Blessing	Blessing	Blessing/Sending

been different levels of commitment to worship among the people of the parish — some attending services regularly, even daily, others once or twice a year or less — but all were considered a part of this single church. This understanding, dating back to very ancient times, was not questioned by the major Reformers, though they recognized and addressed the need to raise the level of understanding and faith among their people.

The more radical Reformers, like Menno Simons in the north of Europe and Michael Sattler further south, taught that every believer had to make a personal confession of faith and be baptized as an adult in order to become a member of the church. The church as the body of believers was understood in this way to be "gathered" out of the world, and to form a separate and godly culture before the eyes of the outside world. It is not hard to see how the proponents of these ideas developed major tensions with those who considered parishes to be sacrosanct. (In fact, these competing ideas of church still cause conflict in some parts of the world today.) But the notions of personal faith and voluntary commitment were destined to become the normative form of Christian community, especially in the New World. Even the Puritan churches would share this tradition in that they were congregational, ruled by the community as a whole and not by any special group of elders or by a bishop.

The dominant characteristic of these (appropriately named) free churches as they developed in America was the belief that personal conversion was the prerequisite not only for church membership but also and more importantly for true worship. Consistent with the inward turn during the Reformation, these Christians emphasized the proper condition of the heart over any outward practice. In addition to the Reformation, they would have been influenced by later movements in Europe, especially by various streams of Pietism and the revivals of John and Charles Wesley. During the seventeenth and eighteenth centuries, believers within larger denominations and state churches in Europe began to meet together in small groups for Bible study and prayer. These Pietist groups often formed small conventicles within larger churches, but occasionally withdrew from these churches to form separate denominations, of which the Moravians and the Brethren are perhaps the best known. These various Pietist streams fed into the free church movement in America. Clearly, these ideas have influenced American culture even outside the walls of the church, contributing to the voluntarism and pluralism that have come to characterize American culture.

When it came to corporate worship, the need for "new birth" or "conversion" was considered necessary, and in this respect free churches often made common cause with the revivalism that we will examine next. Since all who gathered to worship were converted and prepared for worship, it was assumed that everyone should have equal input into how worship was conducted (an attitude that, for better or worse, characterizes much of American Christianity today). Though the authority and preaching of Scripture were central, decisions about what should be included in the service and what should be omitted were made at the grassroots level. Services could even be led by laypeople, who often preached as well. Indeed, pastors were usually laypersons who felt a special call from God to become part of the

regular ministry of the church — a call being, to this day, more important than special training in churches of this style.

Services in the free church style would often be spontaneous and
lively, and in general open to the leading of the Spirit, especially to experiences that would be emotionally moving. In general, this style of
spirituality is distinguished by its emphasis on the need for personal
faith and, often, deeply emotional experiences with God. Accordingly,
experiences that nurture this — private confession and prayer times,
disciplined reading and study of Scripture, and so on — would have
characterized both believers' personal spirituality and their communal worship time, which could itself be described as a kind of family
devotional time. In general, this style of worship reflects a concern for
the community, for mutual edification and encouragement.[3]

Many churches have been influenced by elements of free church
style, especially many Baptist churches and independent Bible
churches in America. Most recently this influence can be seen in the
churches known as Calvary Chapel, founded by Chuck Smith in the
1970s, and in the Vineyard churches, begun by John Wimber somewhat later. These would all agree with a general definition of worship
as practices that promote intimacy with God.

The Revival Style of Worship and Spirituality

One of the places where one could observe the parish form of church
giving way to the gathered church was in Presbyterian Scotland in the
eighteenth century. It was there that the practice of the Holy Fair developed — a weekend or period of days during which people gathered
to prepare themselves for participation in communion.[4] Gradually

---

3. Christopher Ellis sees four values in this tradition: centrality of the Bible, personal faith and piety, concern for community, and an eschatological impulse to see
worship as a sign of the kingdom. See *Gathering: A Theology and Spirituality of Worship in Free-Church Tradition* (London: SCM, 2004).

4. See Leigh E. Schmidt, *Holy Fairs: Scottish Communions and American Revivals
in the Early Modern Period* (Princeton: Princeton University Press, 1989).

the Holy Fair took on the form of a revival, not simply calling people back to faith and repentance in preparation for communion, but calling unbelievers to commit to faith for the first time. This practice was transplanted to America and was hugely influential in the First and Second Great Awakenings in the mid-eighteenth century and the early nineteenth century.

Centered largely in the frontier areas of America, these revivals came to characterize American Christianity in fundamental ways, not least in the area of worship. Prominent among these revivalists was Charles Finney, who in the 1820s instigated what he called "new measures," which were methods of conducting services that would lead people to a place where they would commit themselves to Christ and be converted. These practices issued in liturgical elements that eventually had an impact on the worship style of churches formed during this time. Some of these elements, such as public confession of faith, were part of previous Christian practice placed in this new setting, but others — like the altar call and the extended meeting times — were the products of the revivals themselves, especially as these were developed by Finney and others. The influence of this style of worship extended far beyond the frontier areas where it first developed.

An order of service influenced by this revival style would have begun with prayer and congregational singing. It would have included testimonies of those who had recently come to faith, or come back to faith. The sermon would have resembled others in the Protestant tradition, except that it would have been focused on the invitation to accept Christ, which followed it. Indeed, the whole service and the spirituality it fostered would have centered on the harvest of souls, for which purpose the extended time of invitation and the "anxious bench" were developed. The anxious bench was a pew at the front of the sanctuary where those who fell under the conviction of the Holy Spirit would be invited to sit, until they were ready to come forward to the altar to be converted.

Religious historian Jeanne Kilde points out that at the end of the nineteenth century, this revival tradition of worship went in two directions. On the one hand, it influenced what she calls the home churches of suburban America, which represented the triumph of domestic Christianity. These churches, with padded pews and lounges that resembled living rooms, would encourage unbelievers to come to the church just as one would encourage neighbors to come to one's home. On the other hand, Kilde notes that there were churches that stayed behind in the cities and sought to reach out to the community through urban mission, which, she says, later led to the activist Social Gospel churches of the early twentieth century.[5] One can argue that socially activist churches today continue this revival tradition, although they might be surprised to hear this. Similar to revival services and their call to conversion, activist services (and sermons) are often oriented toward making a decision that will mobilize the congregation to engage in various kinds of social ministry.

The revival style of worship in general and the accompanying spirituality continue to characterize much of American Christianity today, especially in the South — and American missionaries have extended its influence to many parts of the world. Someone visiting African churches, for example, would be impressed with their evangelistic character, an emphasis that African believers take into the whole of their lives. A most interesting contemporary example of the revival style of worship can be seen in what are called "seeker churches." During the 1970s, churches began to realize that many Americans no longer saw Christianity or the church as vital parts of their lives. Churches such as Willow Creek Church in Barrington, Illinois, began to develop services that would attract the attention of these secular and post-Christian people. Since many of these people had negative associations with the traditional church, "seeker churches" often built spaces that omitted any overt reference to Christianity. As in the revivals of earlier periods, everything in the service — the music, the drama and art, the preaching, even the physical arrangement of the worship environment — was integrated into the goal of attracting unchurched people to hear the Gospel in a fresh way, and ultimately to commit themselves to Christ.

5. See Kilde, *When Church Became Theatre,* Chapter Four.

60

The variety of worship styles has also had an influence on church architecture, which in turn made its own contribution to the understanding of worship. In the case of the revival style of worship, the reciprocal influence of space and liturgy can be seen in the famous tabernacles built during the second half of the nineteenth century. Nothing was to impede worshipers from seeing and finally moving toward what came to be called the "altar." (Notice how the terminology changed. The altar was no longer the place where animals were sacrificed, as in the Old Testament, or even the table on which the sacrifice of Christ was remembered, as in the Middle Ages; now it was the place at the front of the church where one came to "give oneself to Christ" — that is, to lay "one's all" on the altar. The worshipers were to consider that, following Christ, they themselves were the sacrifice to be made on this altar.) The influence of this style continues to the present. In Los Angeles, for example, the famous West Angeles Temple, a large African-American congregation of the Church of God, built its imposing worship space in such a way that nothing impeded either the view of the preacher and the platform or, more importantly, the movement of people down toward the altar during the altar call. All the rows of the large amphitheatre converge down at the altar. The worshiping life of the congregation focuses here — worshipers come down to the front to meet God in what is clearly, for them, the central sacramental moment. All the elements of the service are oriented to this end of bringing people to Christ (or back to Christ).

To highlight the continuity of the revival style, Table 2 on page 62 shows the similarities between an order of service influenced by Charles Finney and a contemporary seeker service.

Worship as Christian Nurture

Not all American Christians supported Finney's new measures, or even the dominant revivalism of the American frontier. In 1847, New England preacher Horace Bushnell published a famous book titled *Christian Nurture*, which was intended as a response to this popular revival

Table 2. The Continuity of Revival-Style Worship

Revival-Style Order of Service	Twentieth-Century Seeker Service
Prayer	Welcome and prayer
Praise (congregational singing)	Praise time (often called "worship"); singing praise choruses
Testimony	Presentation (drama, movie clip)
Sermon	Sermon
Invitation: Harvest of Souls	Invitation to come to Christ or to "get involved" in the life of the church

mentality. Rather than insisting on the need for a crisis experience of conversion and arranging religious instruction and worship style accordingly, Bushnell argued that parents and pastors should work so that young people grow up in an atmosphere in which they never know themselves not to be Christian. Bushnell believed this could be generalized into a more appropriate way of forming people in the faith and of encouraging worship. The practices of the Christian home and the sanctuary, the activities that constitute worship, should all focus on *nurturing* faith rather than on triggering it in a moment of crisis.

Clearly, this view would lead to a very different style of spirituality. Rather than seeking to produce an emotional crisis in which one is moved to make a decision, the Christian life should make use of practices that develop faith over a long period of time — indeed, over the whole of one's life. Personal and family devotions would still be important — in fact, the mid- and late nineteenth century featured many prints of young people gathered around (usually) their mother, who was reading to them from Scripture — but the focus would be on nurturing faith over time. Churches formed in this style were the first to institute Sunday schools as a means of developing the faith of young people. Their programs had a didactic dimension to them, and included, interestingly, a (renewed) emphasis on catechism and creeds, printed programs, and a set liturgy.

Later in the nineteenth century, this style was frequently linked to the Gothic Revival in church architecture, which was believed to be the epitome of Christian church form. The preference for the Gothic style reflected the view that certain spaces naturally evoked feelings that were more religious and encouraged appropriate devotion. In this American style more than any other, aesthetics came to play an important role. Believers in this tradition were usually better educated and had an appreciation for art and classical music, which they felt to be auxiliary aids to a worship that nurtures faith over time. This style of spirituality came to be identified with the liberalism of early twentieth-century American Christianity and continues to influence large parts of mainline Christianity.

The Pentecostal Style of Worship

In many ways, Pentecostal worship may be defined as the most influential style of worship in the twentieth century. From its birth in 1907 in Los Angeles, its influence has spread throughout America and the world. Pentecostal worship combines the freedom of the lay-led free church with the call to decision, or, in this case, to the "filling of the Holy Spirit," coming from the revival style. In many ways it represents what might be called a cross-cultural worship style, since critical elements of African-American worship were incorporated through the influence of one of the founders, Pastor William Seymour, a black pastor, during the Azusa Street Revival in Los Angeles. Indeed, its cross-cultural character, and especially its roots in the black church, may account for its popularity in Latin America and especially in Africa.

Theologically, Pentecostal worship was formed under the influence of a Wesleyan and Methodist piety that encouraged experiences of a deeper life in Christ, an emphasis of many eighteenth-century Bible conferences. In the Pentecostal tradition, these deeper experiences of grace came to be interpreted as a baptism of the Holy Spirit, an experience in which believers came to be "filled with the Spirit" and spoke in unknown tongues — what is sometimes called the "initial evidence" of the Spirit's presence. (In the next chapter we will note the way in which this experience came to be conceived as a kind of sacrament.) The emphasis on the Holy Spirit led to an expectation that the gifts of the Spirit would be evident in worship, and therefore created an openness to the manifestations of the Spirit, not only speaking in tongues but also prophesying and even supernatural healing, as a normative part of corporate worship. The expectation of the manifestation of the Spirit in worship had a parallel influence on personal and domestic spirituality, where the ecstatic experience of the Spirit and its manifestation in tongues became common.

The order of service of Pentecostal worship came to reflect much of the revival and free church styles, with the significant difference that spaces in the service (and the sanctuary) would have encouraged the expression of the gifts of the Spirit, and the invitation would have been not only to conversion but also to the experience of being filled with the Holy Spirit. The service of prayer and worship would have been especially lively with the presence of those speaking (or singing) in the Spirit. Its most notable characteristic would have been its spontaneity, resulting from a radical openness to the Spirit. Along with testimonies, there would have been time for those who had a special word of prophecy for the people — though these special words might come at any moment, even in the midst of a pastor's sermon. Sermons would have been lively expositions of Scripture and would have been directed especially to invite people to faith and to experience the fullness of the Holy Spirit. Probably the most pervasive influence of Pentecostalism on American worship has been the introduction of a time of lively singing of contemporary music, often Scripture put to music, at the beginning of the service, which has become virtually normative in what is called contemporary worship.

Despite the diversity of Pentecostalism, one can discern an emerging style of spirituality in the movement — a spirituality that influenced many in the mainline denominations through the charismatic movement in the second half of the twentieth century. The em-

64

phasis on the Holy Spirit being given to all, without discrimination of gender, class, or education, is often accompanied by a strong millennial sense.[6] To Pentecostals, the gifts of the Holy Spirit are clear evidence that we have entered the last days that are predicted in Joel 2 and that Peter spoke of at Pentecost (Acts 2). Furthermore, a Pentecostal spirituality is both communal and inclusive. The celebration of the Spirit draws believers together even as it celebrates these gifts among the last and the least. Perhaps this is one reason why Pentecostal churches have often been born in storefronts or unused warehouses, where all are welcome and a new community of people can spontaneously spring to life. Finally, Pentecostal worship features a fully embodied spirituality: God is praised with raised arms and dancing, and the sick are invited to come for healing.

One of the most prominent contemporary expressions of Pentecostal spirituality is to be found in the so-called third-wave Pentecostalism, which arose in the 1970s and is represented by the Vineyard churches. A leader in Calvary Chapel, John Wimber came to feel that the free church style was too limiting, and he sought a greater experience of the Holy Spirit, giving birth to the Vineyard churches. Although Wimber later resisted some of the extremes to which this movement was prone, he did acknowledge the influence of Pentecostal spirituality, though the influence of Pietism is evident in Vineyard churches as well. Wimber's definition of worship was the pursuit of intimacy with God. He envisioned the development of this intimacy in five phases within the worship service. Professor Barry Liesch has described Wimber's program this way. The invitation phase corresponds to the call to worship, often drawing the people to worship by celebration and hand-clapping. In the engagement phase, worshipers begin to draw near to God, and music is addressed to God rather than to the congregation, as in the previous phase. In the exaltation phase, people begin to sing to God with exclamation and power. In the adoration phase, the dynamics are subdued and the music is slower, reflecting the immanence of God rather than the transcendence, as in the previ-

6. On this, see White, *Protestant Worship,* pp. 199-201.

ous phase. Finally comes the intimacy phase, the quietest and most personal part of the service, where worshipers rest in the presence of God.[7] Like Pentecostalism more generally, Wimber's views (and his writings) have had a large influence on contemporary worship.

Conclusion: The Contemporary Situation

The styles of spirituality discussed here continue their influence in contemporary worship today. And while they exist in multiple forms of mutual influence, I would argue that in one way or another, these major styles have proven critical in the development of worship. Of course, it is often difficult to distinguish the various styles and substyles today, and this fact calls for at least some comment in a short introduction to worship. Along with the styles reviewed here, two historical factors in the twentieth century have proven significant in contemporary developments: the liturgical renewal centered in the Catholic Church, and the revival of evangelical Christianity in the United States in the second half of the twentieth century.

First, the liturgical renewal in the Catholic Church, which began in Belgium in 1909 and is associated with Lambert Beauduin, initiated a century-long period of renewal in Catholic worship. Beauduin's work called for participation of the laity in the liturgy. The liturgy that he was referring to was the traditional Catholic mass, which had gone through its own development since the medieval and Counter-Reformation periods. To Protestants it may not sound revolutionary to call for lay participation in worship, but for Catholics this was an important (and unprecedented) initiative. During the Second Vatican Council (1961-1965), it led to a call for the "full, active, and conscious participation in

7. See Barry Liesch, *The New Worship: Straight Talk on Music and the Church* (Grand Rapids: Baker, 2001), pp. 54-58. Liesch sees three types of services dominating today: the liturgical service, which corresponds to our mainline model; the thematic service, where music and readings serve the sermon, which is probably closest to our description of the Free-Church model; and the free-flowing praise service, where music and sermon are independent, which Liesch sees embodied in Wimber's five-phase proposal.

the liturgy by the whole church" — a church that was being (re)defined as the "Pilgrim people of God." These stirrings were accompanied by a range of developments — including special programs of study at Notre Dame University, and an important group of new writers on spirituality like Thomas Merton and Henri Nouwen — that were to have a profound influence not only on the Catholic Church but on many Protestant groups as well. For Protestants this stimulated a rediscovery of aspects of the Christian tradition that had long been forgotten. Retreats featuring Ignatian spirituality, medieval practices like pilgrimages and processions or praying the labyrinth, Taizé worship (itself an ecumenical development) — all became as popular among many Protestants as they were among Catholics. Clearly, the influence on renewal has gone in both directions. Protestant scholar James White claims that while the initial agenda of the post–World War II liturgical movement in the Catholic Church was largely borrowed from the Protestant churches, since Vatican II the main impulse for renewal in Protestant churches has come largely from Catholic developments.[8]

The second influence to note is the revival of evangelical Christianity in the last half of the twentieth century. After World War II, a new generation of leadership emerged among what was then called fundamentalist Christianity that encouraged a new engagement with the broader culture. This new spirit was represented by fresh theological reflection and new forms of evangelism that made use of contemporary media. This movement among those who came to be called evangelicals issued in a significant period of church growth. Accompanying this was the desire to find new ways of worshiping and expressing the faith that would attract a disengaged, post-Christian culture. A brief list of the many initiatives — the Youth for Christ clubs and the Saturday-night rallies, organizations like Young Life and Focus on the Family, and the many campaigns of Billy Graham — gives some indication of the creativity and openness to change that accompanied this countrywide revival.

This postwar revival, combined with the continuing influence of Pentecostalism in the 1970s and 1980s, gave rise to the development of

---

8. White, *Protestant Worship,* p. 32.

entirely new forms of church structure and worship — what are sometimes called new paradigm churches. While continuing the free church
focus on preaching, these churches often made innovative use of the
arts, especially music. In the early 1970s, for example, Calvary Chapel in
southern California adapted American popular-music styles in Christian love songs that encouraged a meditative, musical reflection on
Scripture and one's life with Christ. Talented composers, many of them
converted in what was called the Jesus movement, began writing music
that by the 1980s had achieved success and visibility in the mainstream
music industry. While music had always been central to Christian worship, the music issuing from this movement can safely be said to have
impacted major segments of Christian worship in America. The common practice of worship including a "worship band," with several individuals with microphones leading congregational singing, surely derives from this movement. Two of the most influential churches in
America — the aforementioned Willow Creek Church and Saddleback
Church in Lake Forest, California — have acknowledged their indebt-
edness to the music birthed in Calvary Chapel.[9]

By the end of the century, the renewal among evangelicals and the
increasingly visible liturgical renewal were to converge in the development of a wide variety of worship forms. We cannot survey all the cross-
cutting influences here, but it is possible to suggest a kind of contemporary typology in three streams. One way that styles of worship can be
sorted out is to ask this question: Where in the service do worshipers
feel that they are closest to God? Or, to put it another way, what part of
the service constitutes a "theophany" — that is, what is the particular
element that communicates the presence of God?[10] Of course, most
worship services will have more than one point at which God is made
available, but all will usually have a single element that carries more
weight in the service than any other. This element may be a focus on

9. I am indebted to private correspondence with Dr. Chuck Fromm for help on
this point.
10. Lester Ruth makes a similar point in his article "A Rose by Any Other Name,"
though he does not use the term "theophanic." He proposes the threefold categori-
zation that I use.

the preaching of the Word in traditional Reformed churches, or a focus on the taking of the Eucharist among Anglican and Catholic congregations. There may be still other events — times of corporate prayer, the experience of speaking in tongues, or the period of time at the beginning of worship when the community sings its prayers — that provide worshipers with access to God. In the Orthodox churches, it is praying before icons — a practice Protestants have long debated and sometimes misunderstood — that especially communicates what are called the "energies" of God's presence for worshipers.

Though it is an oversimplification, one might describe three contemporary streams of worship styles among Protestants in the new century. Each of these has a differing relationship to medieval patterns and, consequently, a different understanding of what is "theophanic" in the service. On the left are those whose services are most distant from the medieval pattern, but who attempt to make the strongest connection with the culture around them. On the right, by contrast, are those who would hold more closely to the traditional patterns of worship and want to stand against any influence from the culture. Those in the middle have somewhat more interest in preserving the ancient pattern, but seek by their obedience to Scripture to transform cultural elements. Professor Lester Ruth suggests that it is possible to see those on the left as frequently (though not always) music-oriented in their worship, often in seeker-friendly services. Those in the center — usually Reformed and Methodist — are Word-oriented. And those on the right are (Eucharistically) table-oriented. That is, those on the left often see music as itself "theophanic," those in the center insist that the Word preached and heard is alone "theophanic," and those on the right believe that God is present in the elements of the Eucharist.[11] (The table on p. 70 roughly corresponds to Ruth's spectrum.)

---

11. Ruth, "A Rose by Any Other Name," pp. 67-71. The terms "left-wing worship" and "right-wing worship" that I am echoing here come from James White, *Protestant Worship*, p. 23. One can say that the three streams of worship discussed here correspond roughly to Liesch's categories: the music-oriented service is what he calls "free-flowing," the Word-oriented service is what he calls "thematic," and the Eucharistic service is what he calls "liturgical." See *The New Worship*, p. 53.

Table 3. The Spectrum of Worship Renewal, 2000-2005

Contemporary Movements

Seeker-Sensitive Worship	Contemporary Worship	Blended Worship	Emergent Church	Liturgical Renewal

Influences

Revival tradition, Willow Creek Church	Vineyard churches, Hillsong Church, *Worship Leader* magazine	Various	Multiple, Internet-driven	Vatican II, Notre Dame

(music-oriented) - - - - - - - - - - *(Word- and table-oriented)* - - - - - - - - - - - *(table-oriented)*

Of course, the reality of contemporary worship is far more complex than this. But it is safe to say that all the various styles of worship would fit somewhere along a spectrum that would seek to find some relation between the tradition of worship that we reviewed in the last chapter and the longings and styles of contemporary culture. Those on the left will inevitably be more open to cultural forms, while those on the right will be more insistent on the traditional forms. One might venture a spectrum like the one presented in Table 3 above.

This variety is either perplexing or invigorating, depending on one's perspective. But it does speak of the vitality of American Christianity, because the influence of these movements of renewal extends far beyond the evangelical and Catholic groups in which they began. One can easily find groups within evangelical and Catholic circles that are radically opposed to the innovations represented by these renewals, but one can also see the influence of these impulses more broadly in mainline Protestantism.

The relevant point, and the intended focus of this chapter, is that the resulting styles of worship, whether they continue traditional forms or depart from them in significant ways, when shaped into particular worship practices, form us as God's people. We are shaped differently by the various practices represented — differently, but not, we hope and pray, antagonistically. For, while it is certainly true that none of the movements mentioned has any particular corner on true worship, and all in some ways will reflect various weaknesses, together they make up (along with Catholic and Orthodox traditions that we have not discussed),[12] insofar as it is available to us, the complete heritage of the people of God. And while we all find ourselves rooted in some particular place along this spectrum, we pray for the grace to be open to aspects of God's truth that may be found elsewhere. The diversity itself is a tribute to the various ways that Christianity has been able to adapt itself to culture and circumstance throughout its history. Clearly, renewal in worship often encourages diversity and experimentation. As James White notes, "The purpose of worship reform is not the elimination of multiplicity or the achievement of administrative efficiency. It is simply to enable people to worship with deeper commitment and participation — which may require more denominations and traditions rather than fewer ones."[13]

In the next chapter we turn to the theological underpinnings of worship to explore the renewal in theology that has accompanied this renewal in worship, recognizing that both are significant, in part, because they have so often been deeply ecumenical. Of course, to call attention to its ecumenical character is enough to cause some among both Catholics and Protestants to dismiss worship renewal out of hand. But my purpose is not to promote some particular form of ecumenicity so much as to call attention to the way that current discussions of worship are re-integrating aspects of worship that have been for centuries estranged from each other. These movements are also important because they provide us with the tools to balance our concern for cultural rootedness with our aspiration to biblical and historical faithfulness.

12. Good introductions to these traditions are Keith F. Pecklers, *Worship: A Primer in Christian Ritual* (Collegeville, Minn.: Liturgical Press, 2003), and John Fenwick, *The Eastern Orthodox Liturgy* (Bramcote: Grove Books, 1978).

13. White, *Protestant Worship*, p. 213.

SUGGESTIONS FOR FURTHER READING

Simon Chan. *Liturgical Theology: The Church as Worshiping Community.* Downers Grove, Ill.: InterVarsity Press, 2007.

Eddie Gibbs and Ryan K. Bolger. *Emerging Churches: Creating Christian Community in Postmodern Cultures.* Grand Rapids: Baker Academic, 2005.

Todd Johnson, ed. *The Conviction of Things Not Seen.* Grand Rapids: Brazos Press, 2002.

Jeanne Kilde. *When Church Became Theatre: The Transformation of Evangelical Architecture and Worship in Nineteenth-Century America.* Oxford: Oxford University Press, 2002.

Mark A. Torgerson. *An Architecture of Immanence: Architecture for Worship and Ministry Today.* Grand Rapids: William B. Eerdmans, 2007.

James F. White. *Protestant Worship: Traditions in Transition.* Louisville: Westminster John Knox, 1989.

QUESTIONS FOR DISCUSSION

1. Reflect on the tradition of spirituality in which you were raised (or into which you were introduced at conversion). What are its strengths and weaknesses?

2. Do you agree with the assertion that some external forms are "necessary" to Christian worship? Why or why not?

3. "There is no biblical tradition of spirituality." Discuss why this statement might be true or false.

4. Discuss the recovery of the historical streams of spirituality in relation to the multicultural nature of the church today. Is emphasizing these traditions limiting for younger churches? Should we be speaking of "Kenyan worship" or "Latin American spirituality"? Why or why not?

5. Discuss how you think theological traditions are related to traditions of spirituality. Is part of our problem with worship today that the latter has not been properly informed by the former?

CHAPTER 4

Holy, Holy, Holy

The Trinitarian Character of Worship

Standing to sing a hymn, listening to Scripture being read, hearing the pastor pray for the needs of the congregation   all the activities of worship, however routine they may become, are nevertheless a way of doing theology. The practices of worship, I would argue, are a central means by which God forms us according to the story of Jesus Christ, by the power of the Holy Spirit. There are two theological components implied in this definition that we will explore in this and the following chapters. In this chapter I will argue that the basic structure of worship is Trinitarian — that worship is initiated and enabled by the persons of the Trinity, and, further, that worship results in believers being enabled to actually share in the Trinitarian life of God. While various groups of Christians would emphasize a particular aspect of the structure and the story, all would endorse this Trinitarian structure and the Jesus story in some way, and it is this broad area of agreement that I seek to explore here. But this sharing can also be described as being shaped by a particular narrative. Worship itself has a particular narrative shape — what Christians refer to as the "Gospel" or the story of Jesus Christ. This storied dimension of worship will be the focus of the following chapter. Then, in the succeeding chapter, I will describe ways in which this narrative structure results in a community formed by a particular "polity," or way of life.

Notice that we come to discuss a central teaching of the Christian faith, the Trinity, only after we have explored the various activities that constitute worship. It is quite intentional that this chapter comes at the very center of our discussion of worship, showing its critical importance. But still, it comes *after* the discussion of things Christians do week by week in their services of worship. Does this mean that it is somehow less important than these practices? Not at all. You will remember that, in the brief discussion about theology in the introduction, I described an idea that is widely accepted among theologians: that the life of worship embodies what is called primary theology. Believers express their fundamental beliefs, in the first instance, not by explaining them in propositions but by embodying them in devotional acts — prayer, praise, Bible study, and so on. Theological reflection developed by theologians and studied in theology classes is secondary theology, which usually takes the shape of a critical and systematic reflection on the worshiping life of God's people as they read Scripture together. If this is true, the teaching of the church, what is called doctrine (literally, "what is taught"), finds its first and fundamental expression in the liturgy — in the worship of God's people.

How Trinitarian Worship Shapes Theological Reflection

Earlier I pointed out that the activities of worship are prior to systematic reflection, both historically and personally. Historically, the faith of early Christians in the divinity of Christ, and later the Trinity, found its initial expression in worship — in the prayers, the preaching, the creeds, and the catechetical preparation for baptism — before this was formulated systematically by the great councils. But this is true personally as well. We experience the Trinitarian structure of worship in our praying, our recital of creeds, and our reading and hearing of Scripture before we can formulate these practices in any systematic way — if, indeed, we are ever able to do this. Understanding is more often a product of belief and practice than the reverse, as St. Augustine taught: we believe and confess in order to understand. At the same time, we seek understanding in order to become better believers and confessors. Even if the goal of theology is right worship and right living, understanding is not unimportant. Indeed, all our devotional activity implies some conception of theology, as I have emphasized. And growth in understanding and careful reflection on what happens when we pray or take communion will surely enrich and encourage our worship life. There is ample evidence for the barrenness that results from either unthinking practice or unengaged theology. The goal of this chapter is to illumine the connection between these important activities from the side of systematic understanding.

We see the priority of worship, and the language of worship, at work already in the worship of the New Testament church. The first issue that early Christians faced was how Jesus should be addressed in worship. How does one speak in a way that holds together Christ's earthly and divine identity? The resulting formula, "Jesus is Lord," became the first Christian confession — at least among Greek-speaking Christians. This also became the starting point for reflection on the Trinity, since it implied that Jesus was a person in intimate relation with, but distinct from, God the Father. It was a bold pronouncement because it identified Jesus with the Old Testament Yahweh. It was also a daring political statement: Since Jesus is Lord, Caesar is not! This brief confession was the starting point for a centuries-long discussion on the exact nature of Christ, the relation between his human and his divine nature, and eventually Christ's relationship to God and the Holy Spirit. Theologians and historians have pointed out the ways in which the worshiping life of the church was the context where these issues were first worked out — especially in the developing baptismal creeds.[1]

The centrality of Christ in Christian worship grows out of not only the way in which Christ brought together the human and the divine, but also the way in which he connects heaven and earth. Here theologians have long recognized the centrality of the Ascension in Christian worship. In ascending to heaven after his resurrection, Christ not

---

1. The classic study of these issues is J. N. D. Kelly, *Early Christian Creeds,* 3rd ed. (London: Longman, 1972).

only completed the redemptive work of the cross but also anticipated believers' own participation in the glory of heaven. Swiss Reformed theologian J. J. von Allmen argues that it is best to think of the movement of Christ's life, death, and resurrection and ascension as a kind of liturgical process: "The ascension is not only a royal procession, as we are too easily inclined to believe. It is also a liturgical procession; in ascending to heaven, Jesus enters into the heavenly sanctuary."[2]

So it is no surprise that in the early church the struggle to develop an appropriate language for worship focused in the first place on the person of Christ. Early Christians saw themselves first and last as disciples of Jesus Christ. Clearly, for Christians, Christ is the entry point into both our life *with* God and, eventually, our life *in* God. Paul seems to be arguing this point in Galatians 4:4-6 and Romans 8:14-17. In the first passage, Paul is pointing out how Christians come to be adopted as children of God. He writes, "Because you are children, God has sent the Spirit of his Son into our hearts, crying, 'Abba! Father!' So you are no longer a slave but a child, and if a child then also an heir, through God" (vv. 6-7). Paul is alluding to the central aspect of Jesus' own consciousness: his awareness of intimacy with the Father, expressed by his well-known use of "Abba" (see Matt. 11:25-30 and Mark 14:36).

When early Christians began to recognize their own intimacy with God on the basis of their faith in Christ, they realized that they were being moved by the Spirit to speak the same "Abba" that Christ himself spoke. So Paul says in Romans 8, "When we cry, 'Abba! Father!' it is that very Spirit bearing witness with our spirit that we are children of God, and if children, then heirs, heirs of God and joint heirs with Christ" (vv. 15-17). Notice that the involvement of the Spirit enables us to address God as Father, as Christ himself did. It is this theological movement that is facilitated by the practices of worship — in the prayers, the creeds, and the singing, believers are encouraged to address God directly as Father, and in so doing grow in their awareness of being God's children.

2. J. J. von Allmen, *Worship: Its Theology and Practice* (New York: Oxford University Press, 1965), p. 25.

Exploring the Trinitarian Structure of Worship

In the practices of worship, then, week in and week out, the Trinitarian character of God is implanted in worshipers' minds and hearts — and, as we will see in the following chapters, on the quality of everyday life as well. Worship enables and sustains Christians as they seek to become bearers of the likeness of Christ. Christians understand this process of growth in various ways. Most Protestants refer to it as the process of sanctification; Catholics understand it in terms of conversion; Orthodox call it deification, the way that believers become like God. But all would agree that this process begins in worship, is nurtured in worship, and, at the end of all things, finds its culmination in the worship of heaven.

There are several ways that one might describe the Trinitarian character of worship.[3] One might discuss the way that worship, initiated by God, enabled by God, and directed back to God, has an essentially Trinitarian structure — that is, the way worship reflects the inner Trinitarian life of God. Another approach is to emphasize the relational character of worship as reflecting the relations within the Trinity. Worship, as von Allmen points out, is an emphatic denial of human solitude and the site of true community: "Because Christ is present, all those whom he has saved are present also."[4] In this sense worship reflects the relational character of God and places worshipers in a vital relationship with God and with each other. Picking up on the concrete revelation of the Trinity in salvation history — what is called the "economic Trinity" — one might emphasize the way that this Trinitarian story is reiterated in worship, the approach we will follow in the next chapter. Though in some sense all of these emphases ought to inform our thinking, our emphasis in what follows here is the way the Trinitarian character of God impacts our imagination, proposing a "vision" of life that human beings are called to imitate. The argument is that wor-

3. Five such approaches are reviewed in John Witvliet, "The Trinitarian DNA of Christian Worship: Perennial Themes in Recent Theological Literature," *Colloquium: Music, Worship, Arts* (New Haven: Yale Institute of Music, 2004).

4. von Allmen, *Worship: Its Theology and Practice*, p. 198.

ship is the place where this "image" is displayed clearly — where, indeed, this image is *communicated* to worshipers. We will describe this image in the following three ways: as seeking the glory of God, as invited and enabled by Christ, and as empowered by the Holy Spirit.

The Gift of the Glory of God

Glory is one of the richest concepts that Scripture uses to describe the life and character of God, and eventually to describe the believer's participation in that life. Its fundamental meaning is an abundance, or honor and splendor that become visible in some way — the aesthetic component of glory, its visibility, is never far from the surface. Anglican theologian Christopher Cocksworth calls it the "visible and tangible evidence of wealth, personality, and power . . . [the] sensory impact of the invisible God."[5]

Note first that this is a fundamental characteristic of God: it belongs to God and accompanies all that God does. It was evident in the creation of both the human person (Ps. 8:5) and nature (Ps. 19:1). In the wilderness wanderings, the glory of the Lord appeared in a cloud (Exod. 16:10); God's glory filled the temple at its dedication so that the priests could not enter (1 Kings 8:11); and one day God's glory will be manifest so that all will see it (Isa. 40:5). God's glory was especially evident in the life of Christ: at his birth (Luke 2:14), at his transfiguration (Matt. 17:2), and, incomprehensibly, at his death (John 13:31). How the sufferings of Christ could manifest God's glory is a fundamental mystery that, as we will see, still troubles the church.

But a further aspect of God's glory, one we will specially focus on, is the inclination that God has to share his glory, to see it reflected in the created order and in those who hear and obey his Word. The inclination to share this glory expresses the reality of God's self-giving love. Paul is specifically referring to worship practices in Second Co-

5. Christopher Cocksworth, *Holy, Holy, Holy: Worshipping the Trinitarian God* (London: Darton, Longman & Todd, 1997), p. 127.

78

rinthians when he discusses the Christian's participation in God's glory. Often, Paul says, when the Book of Moses (the part of the Hebrew Scripture called the Torah) is read in the synagogue, there is a veil over those who hear. As ancient Israel was unable to see the glory of God when Moses came down from the mountain with the law, so there was a veil over the eyes of people in Paul's day that kept them from seeing the glory of God. Only in Christ is this veil set aside (2 Cor. 3:14). When one turns to Christ — and here the practices of worship are central — this veil is removed, and one can see the glory.

The Trinitarian aspect of this process becomes clear when Paul declares, "Where the Spirit of the Lord is, there is freedom. And all of us, with unveiled faces, seeing the glory of the Lord as though reflected in a mirror, are being transformed into the same image from one degree of glory to another; for this comes from the Lord, the Spirit" (3:17-18). The implication is that when Christ has removed the veil from our eyes, we are able, by the Spirit, to progressively "see" the glory of the Lord through the Word of God that is read and expounded in the assembly. Furthermore, this illumination results in the ongoing transformation of worshipers from one degree of glory to another.

The individual who best describes this reality is the eighteenth-century American preacher and theologian Jonathan Edwards. Edwards specially emphasizes the way that God's love moves him to make visible this glory first in creation and then in the new creation, the church. In his classic work *The End for Which God Created the World,* he writes,

> When God was about to create the world, he had respect to that emanation of his glory. . . . He had regard to it as an emanation from himself, a communication of himself, and, as the thing communicated in its nature returned to himself, as its final term. And he had regard to it also as the emanation was to the creature, and as the thing communicated was in the creature, as its subject.[6]

6. From *The End for Which God Created the World,* in *The Works of Jonathan Edwards: Ethical Writings,* ed. Paul Ramsey, vol. 8 in *The Works of Jonathan Edwards,* ed. John E. Smith (New Haven: Yale University Press, 1989), p. 532.

Edwards is elaborating the Pauline teaching that all things come from God and are of God and will eventually return to God. But Edwards elaborates this process of communication in terms of what he calls "emanation." For Edwards, created reality is a network of dispositional powers, what he calls "habits," that are grounded in God. But this ground is characterized by a dynamic impulse toward self-communication existing within the Godhead because of God's love, and extending outside of God in the creation as emanation. Theologian Sang Hyun Lee expresses it this way: "Created existence . . . is the spatio-temporal repetition of God's inner Trinitarian fullness."[7] This communication of God in an important sense centers on the human creature, repeating in the creature something of the fullness of God.

Edwards's reference to the creature refers here ultimately to Christ, who is the highest expression of God's emanation and communication of glory. Edwards connects this expression of glory with the highest (what he calls "primary") beauty, so that sharing in Christ is at the same time a sharing in the beauty which is God's glory. Human desire and the general attraction of beauty (usually through what Edwards calls "secondary beauty") are manifestations of this deeper longing to share in God's nature. As theologian Graham Ward puts it, "The apprehension of the beauty of God is the constitution of beauty itself."[8] But as Ward goes on to say, this experience of beauty is never direct: it is always mediated, in the first instance by Christ as the express image of God's beauty, and in the second instance by the forms that communicate this. Edwards describes this in terms of God's communication of himself in Christ:

> For God having from eternity from his infinite goodness designed to communicate himself to creatures, the way in which he designed

7. Sang Hyun Lee, *The Philosophical Theology of Jonathan Edwards* (Princeton: Princeton University Press, 1988), p. 173.

8. Graham Ward, "The Beauty of God," in John Milbank, Graham Ward, and Edith Wyschogrod, *Theological Perspectives on God and Beauty* (Harrrisburg, Pa.: Trinity Press, 2003), p. 58.

to communicate himself to elect beloved creatures, all of them, was to unite himself to a created nature, and to become one of the creatures, and to gather together in one all elect creatures in that creature that he assumed into a personal union with himself, and to manifest to them and maintain intercourse with them through him.[9]

So, in the experience of the believer's union with Christ, the glory or beauty of God is fully known and shared. This was God's purpose in creating the world: to form it as a communication of divine love, a dynamic network of dispositions manifest as beauty. As Edwards says,

> Thus it is easy to conceive how God should seek the good of the creature, consisting in the creature's knowledge and holiness, and even his happiness, for a supreme regard to himself; as his happiness arises from that which is an image and participation of God's own beauty; and consists in the creature's exercising a supreme regard to God and complacence in him; in beholding God's glory, in esteeming and loving it, and rejoicing in it, and in his exercising and testifying love and supreme respect to God: which is the same thing with the creature's exalting God as his chief good, and making him his supreme end.[10]

This is deep and complex theology, but it essentially provides an expanded description of what happens to believers who gather to worship God. Indeed, one could not ask for a more complete description of the theological process that is embodied in the practices of worship. These are meant to mediate the very goodness of God that is supremely manifested in Jesus Christ, which image we behold in worship, and in beholding come ourselves to share. I will argue below that, in general, there is no other way that this divine reality can be fully experienced than through those various practices by which the

---

9. From *The Works of Jonathan Edwards: The "Miscellanies,"* ed. Ava Chamberlain, vol. 18 in *The Works of Jonathan Edwards,* ed. John E. Smith (New Haven: Yale University Press, 2000), p. 389.

10. Edwards, *The End for Which God Created the World,* p. 533.

believer approaches God. But here I underline the fact that in and through these actions we enjoy, and by the Spirit come even to partake of, the beauty of God that is God's glory. Worship, then, is the conscious participation of believers in the communication of God's glory to and in the world, and in engaging in these practices, worshipers anticipate the final revelation of this glory at the end of history. This is the New Testament vision of worship that we are invited to share.

Participation in God's Glory, Invited and Enabled by Christ

Edwards stressed that Christ became human in order to reveal God in the created order — the beauty of the morning sunrise, of valleys and mountains, or even of a great work of art, he thinks, is a secondary reflection of that beauty which is seen even more clearly in Christ. Indeed, Graham Ward says, because of Christ, who is God communicated to the creature, there is "nothing that cannot be made to tender its beauty as the beauty of God."[11] But this also means that the purpose of Christ's coming is to reveal the Trinitarian character of God. To say this is not simply to insist that God is somehow one and yet three. We will note below that one of the most exciting aspects of recent Trinitarian study is the insight it provides into the dynamic, interrelational character of God, and its intrinsic relation to devotional and mystical practices. Theologians have recently recovered and elaborated the ancient patristic notion that God is a *perichoresis* of mutual love. *Perichoresis* comes from Greek words that together mean "to dance around in chorus"; the word has come to be used to describe the mutual self-giving within the Godhead. The image reflects the mutual interrelationality of God and, beyond this, the aesthetic and Eucharistic (i.e., thanksgiving) character of Trinitarian life. This image represents the most fundamental assertion one can make

11. Ward, "The Beauty of God," p. 62. To deny this, he says, is to see the world as opaque (p. 36).

about the character of the Christian God: the nature of God is a dynamic movement of love and beauty.

Christ came to make present in creation the fullness of this living and loving God. It is the dynamic, charismatic movement of the Trinity that Christ displays in his life, his teaching, and his death and resurrection. As Christopher Cocksworth stresses, "The eternal Son became incarnate in order to reproduce the pattern of his obedient self-giving to the Father through the Spirit *as a human being.*"[12] In John's expressive terminology, the mutual self-giving that characterizes the Trinity from eternity has been manifest — we have seen, heard, and handled it! (1 John 1:1-4). God's purpose of seeing this same dynamic reality reproduced in the believer is grounded first of all in its personal presence in Jesus Christ: because it exists already in Christ, it can exist in the believer who comes to share in Christ's life. Cocksworth notes that this "attitude of Christ on the cross — his giving of himself in obedient response — is replicated in us because it was the basis of his earthly life and remains the basis of his heavenly existence."[13]

The theologian who expresses this purpose of Christ most clearly is the reformer John Calvin. Christ became human, Calvin stressed again and again, to bring humanity up to God. He makes this point near the beginning of his *Institutes:*

> For from the time that Christ was manifested in the flesh, he has been called the Son of God, not only in that he was the eternal Word begotten before all ages from the Father, but because he took upon himself the person and office of the Mediator, that he might join us to God. . . . And certainly for this reason Christ descended to us, to bear us up to the Father, and at the same time to bear us up to himself, inasmuch as he is one with the Father.[14]

---

12. Cocksworth, *Holy, Holy, Holy,* p. 155, his emphasis. See also the following page.

13. Cocksworth, *Holy, Holy, Holy,* p. 161.

14. John Calvin, *Institutes of the Christian Religion,* trans. Ford Lewis Battles, ed. John T. McNeill (Philadelphia: Westminster Press, 1960), 1.13.24; 1.13.26. Subsequent references to this work will be made parenthetically in the text.

In Calvin's view of worship, Christ is made present uniquely in the event of the preached Word. But this Word must not only be preached aright; it must also be heard — that is, received in faith. Calvin, in fact, understood the church to be that place where the Word is preached *and* heard — both were necessary for the reality of the church to be present. But the place where the worshiper is specially joined to Christ, in Calvin's view, is in the sacrament of communion, when the Spirit lifts the believer up to be joined with Christ, who sits at the right hand of the Father. This is the central import of the Eucharist for Calvin. In the preached Word, Christ is clearly pictured as crucified for us; in taking the elements of communion, the believer is "Spiritually" joined with Christ's glorified body in heaven. And it is important to recall here that this joining is not simply for the sake of a mystical union — though it surely includes this — but so that the pattern of mutual self-giving that characterizes the Trinity becomes reflected in the believer's life as well.

To anticipate briefly what we describe in the next chapter, this divine activity is replicated in the actions that make up the narrative of worship. And the believer imaginatively enters this narrative week by week. But note that indwelling this narrative implies the transformation of the believer's life narrative as well. Worship is the redefining of the self, and the story of the self, according to the concrete pattern that God exhibits and that Christ embodies. Again, Calvin describes this beautifully:

> We are not our own: let not our reason nor our will, therefore, sway our plans and deeds. We are not our own: let us therefore not set it as our goal to seek what is expedient for us according to the flesh. We are not our own: insofar as we can, let us therefore forget ourselves and all that is ours. Conversely, we are God's: let us therefore live for him and die for him. We are God's: let his wisdom and will therefore rule all our actions. We are God's: let all the parts of our life accordingly strive toward him as our only lawful goal. (3.7.1)

This marvelous statement develops further Calvin's particular notion of "piety" that we explored earlier. As we noted, it also carries with it a special sense of "service," which for Calvin, as for Paul, was sometimes synonymous with worship. Calvin believed that service or worship means "that a man depart from himself in order that he may apply the whole force of his ability in the service of the Lord. I call 'service' not only what lies in obedience to God's Word, but what turns the mind of man, empty of its own carnal sense, wholly to the bidding of God's Spirit" (3.7.1).

For Calvin, as for most Protestants, the motivation for this calling is the love that was shown to us in Christ's work on the cross. Worship responds to the love and beauty of God that are displayed for the world in the cross. Protestant theologian Belden Lane has described how Calvin believed that worship expresses the yearning and desire of all creation for wholeness — it is a "performance of desire."[15] Worship expresses this desire in a double sense, first in that worshipers know by experience, and thus share in, the pain and disorder that sin has caused. The desire for wholeness moves believers to come to God in the service of worship in the first place, for succor and healing. As the psalmist knew, the sanctuary of the Lord is precisely the place where this painful desire for wholeness can be articulated, both in prayer and in lament.

But worship is the expression of desire in the second sense that it points to and grows out of Christ's work on the cross — the cosmic event that has re-oriented the world on its theological axis. Here the proper sense in which Christ's death can be said to express God's glory comes into focus. John notes that when Jesus went out from the Upper Room on the night he was betrayed, he said emphatically, "Now the Son of Man has been glorified, and God has been glorified in him" (John 13:31). In his commentary on this passage, Calvin notes that in this event a great dramatic reversal has taken place. A world that was disordered and thrown into confusion has been restored. In the cross of Christ, Calvin says, "the whole world has been renewed,

---

15. Belden Lane, "Spirituality as the Performance of Desire: Calvin on the World as a Theatre for the Glory of God," *Spiritus: A Journal of Christian Spirituality* 1, no. 1 (2001): 1-30.

and everything restored to good order."[16] Thus the praise, prayer, preaching, and sacraments of worship all express the longing of creation for the complete revelation of this glory in Christ (Rom. 8:19-23), which was seen most clearly in his death.

For various historical and theological reasons, when it comes to the person of Christ, the emphasis in Protestant worship has almost exclusively been on his death. Believers are called to respond to Christ in love and gratitude because of what he has done for us. One might say that the Protestant emphasis in Christology is typically transactional — on *what* Christ has done for them on the cross — rather than substantial — on *who* Christ is, though Protestant believers often develop a deep, even mystical identification with Christ on this basis, and they can speak eloquently of Christ's divinity. As a result, Protestant believers, especially those influenced by the Reformed tradition, tend to rejoice over what was accomplished on the cross rather than what was represented in the entire life of Christ, from birth clear through to the ascension to God's right hand. Other parts of the Christian family — Orthodox and, to a certain extent, Roman Catholics — have focused more on the substantial nature of Christ as "creature" and thus more on the fact and implication of the Incarnation itself. We cannot develop this further here, but it is already clear that this difference results in different attitudes and distinct practices in worship. Protestants focus more on the narrative of Christ's work and therefore on the resulting narrative of the Christian life — the pattern that we will follow in this book. Orthodox and Catholic worshipers tend to focus more on the eternal deity of Christ and the mystical, timeless identification with this through the practices of worship. This latter emphasis allows theologians like Graham Ward, whom we have quoted previously, to speak of our participation in Christ and the creature's participation in God — a participation best imaged in the Eucharist.

An example of the Catholic focus on the Incarnation can be seen in the work of Hans Urs von Balthasar, a later twentieth-century Catholic

---

16. *Calvin's Commentaries: The Gospel of John,* ed. and trans. William Pringle (Grand Rapids: William B. Eerdmans, 1949), p. 73.

theologian who focused on the aesthetic implications of Christ's life. He too stressed the theological reality of God entering into the created order as the starting point for understanding Christ's work, and therefore for the way he is to be worshiped: "Beyond all creaturely hopes and expectations . . . the revelation in Christ was to bring together in one divine and human Head everything heavenly and earthly, which is thus endowed by grace with a crown the radiance of whose glory, belonging to the Kyrios of the world, was to shed its rays over the whole of creation."[17] On this view, if the glory of creation has been reconstituted in Christ, worship can be the celebration of the gifts of creation as these have been restored by Christ. A legitimate focus of worship, then, is the objects and elements of the created order that, in their beauty, can offer their own hymn of praise to God. We will return to this theme at the end of this chapter and later in Chapter Seven.

Spiritual Formation Empowered by the Holy Spirit

I have stressed that the spiritual formation occasioned by the practices of worship is finally dependent on the work of the Holy Spirit. This results from the Spirit's place in the Trinity as "proceeding from the Father and the Son" — that is, expressing and embodying the wisdom and power of the other members of the Godhead. This is consistent with the special role that the Spirit plays, throughout Scripture, of renewing and restoring creation to its God-appointed purposes. In his Upper Room discourse, Christ makes special reference to the role of Spirit, whom he will send when he returns to the Father. Jesus tells the disciples about the Spirit in John 14: "I will ask the Father, and he will give you another Advocate, to be with you forever. This is the Spirit of truth, whom the world cannot receive, because it neither sees him nor knows him. You know him, because he abides with you, and he will be

---

17. Hans Urs von Balthasar, *The Glory of the Lord: A Theological Aesthetics,* vol. 1: *Seeing the Form,* trans. Erasmo Leiva-Merikakis, ed. Joseph Fessio and John Riches (Edinburgh: T&T Clark, 1982), p. 431.

in you" (vv. 16-17). Christ's promise is fulfilled when the Spirit is poured out on the church at Pentecost, as recounted in Acts 2, an event accompanied by manifestations of power and speaking in unknown tongues. Luke makes clear in the book of Acts that the Spirit continues the work of Jesus in the formation of the church: the journeys of Acts, prompted by the Spirit, are meant to reflect and reiterate the journey of Christ to Jerusalem in the Gospel of Luke.

The work of the Spirit is especially evident in the worship of God's people. The Spirit has a special connection to the Word taught and preached (Eph. 6:17), and to the baptism of believers (1 Cor. 12:13). A particularly important reference to the Spirit's work in worship is Romans 8:26, where Paul notes that the Spirit makes up for our weakness, specifically for our inability to pray properly: "Likewise the Spirit helps us in our weakness; for we do not know how to pray as we ought, but that very Spirit intercedes with sighs too deep for words." So the Spirit's connection to worship in general and to prayer in particular is deep and intimate.

The Spirit also makes concrete through the worshiping experience of God's people the events of the story of Christ — past, present, and future. We have noted that at communion, in Calvin's view, the Spirit lifts the believer to join with Christ. Similarly, in our baptism the Spirit joins us with the death and resurrection of Christ, which we re-experience in that sacrament. As Paul says, "Therefore we have been buried with him by baptism into death, so that, just as Christ was raised from the dead by the glory of the Father, so we too might walk in newness of life" (Rom. 6:4). But the Spirit not only recalls and re-presents events of the past but also anticipates the future. The Spirit is called the down payment of heaven, or the first fruits of the heavenly inheritance. For, like creation, Paul says, we too, "who have the first fruits of the Spirit, groan inwardly while we wait for adoption, the redemption of our bodies" (Rom. 8:23). Again, the stress is on the special role of the Spirit in the renewal of creation, what Paul calls elsewhere the New Creation (2 Cor. 5:17), which is anticipated and celebrated in worship.

It is possible to argue that in the last century God has empowered the Pentecostal movement specifically to remind the church of the role and ministry of the Holy Spirit, especially of its role in worship. Pentecostal worship reminds us that coming before God is first of all a Spirit-directed event, something that God does in and with his people, by the Spirit, that reflects and, in mysterious ways, reiterates events that are rooted in God and anchored in history. Under the influence of the Pentecostal worship style, various kinds of contemporary worship can often reflect something of the spontaneity and drama of worship in the early church. While sometimes this worship can appear more Binitarian than Trinitarian — stressing the Spirit and Christ, but less often the presence of the Father — Pentecostal practice often reflects more of the dynamic of God's presence than many other styles of worship.

What is clear is that in Pentecostal churches — and, we might add, in Black churches in America and Pentecostal-like churches in Africa — many believers enjoy the reality of the presence of God through special manifestations of the gifts of the Spirit: prophesying and speaking in tongues (glossolalia). Indeed, these practices have expanded the lexicon of the practices of worship in important ways.

Recent writers in this tradition have stressed how these special manifestations of the Spirit can become sacramental moments for believers in these churches. That is, they can mediate the living presence of God in powerful ways. Amos Yong, a young Pentecostal theologian, has argued that glossolalia is more than simply a sign of God's presence, though it is surely also that. For the mature Pentecostal believer, this experience is a "vision of the divine life. Glossolalia is now an embodiment of the divine unity, and offers precisely an avenue into participation in the divine life through the divine language. Glossolalia is transformed into divine praise (Acts 10:46), unutterable groans (Rom. 8:26), and the language of angels (1 Cor. 13:1). The Pentecostal, while both enthusiast and proclaimer, is now first and foremost worshiper."[18]

18. Amos Yong, " 'Tongues of Fire' in the Pentecostal Imagination: The Truth of Glossolalia in Light of R. C. Neville's Theory of Religious Symbolism," *Journal of Pentecostal Theology* 12 (1998): 57.

Thus, for Pentecostals it is possible that the particular experience of being filled with the Holy Spirit, as a focus of worship, becomes a sacramental experience that might be compared to the transformation of the body of Christ in the Catholic mass, and to the preaching of the Word in the Protestant tradition. It is this particular practice by which believers are able not only to experience the divine life, but also, by this same Spirit, to participate in it.

Conclusion

The awareness of being in the presence of God, by means of our union with Christ, through the Spirit, is the fundamental structure, the backbone of the worship experience. It may be that this structure is more often implicit than explicit. In practice, worship may appear to be Unitarian or Binitarian, but the reality must always be Trinitarian if we are to truly experience the Triune shape of grace. We will see that the practices of worship — the call to worship, praise, the offering, preaching, sending, and so on — are all Trinitarian activities.

But there is an important point that must be made here to prepare for the conversation that follows in the next chapters. Human beings, because of their finite and embodied nature, do not have immediate access to God. The human approach to God is always *mediated*. This mediation is theological in the first instance, of course — we come to God *through* the incarnate God, Jesus Christ. But as embodied creatures of history, we also come to God in a way that is historically mediated, through the events of the life of Israel, Christ, and the early church. Notice, however, that this "story of Jesus Christ" is not something separate from the Trinitarian life of God that we have reviewed in this chapter; it is the expression of that very life. These events of history, insofar as they are manifestations of God, are what theologians call the "economic Trinity." But how precisely are these external, historical events related to the life of God within the Godhead?

One of the important advances in theological understanding in the twentieth century was to see more deeply the connection between the economic Trinity and the immanent Trinity — that is, between the works of God outside of God (i.e., God's actions in history) and the works, or the relational dynamic of God, within the Godhead — the perichoretic mutuality. Catholic theologian Karl Rahner was the one who advanced the conversation in the sharpest way with his famous declaration that the economic Trinity *is* the immanent Trinity. Protestant theologian Jürgen Moltmann went further in declaring that the cross was itself an event within the life of God. Subsequent theologians have retreated from this attempt to identify the events of history with God's own life — which was seen to lead in the direction of pantheism or at least panentheism (the belief that everything is God or everything is *in* God). But these conversations have provided a deeper sense of the vital connection between God's acts and God's person — that God, as Trinity, is present in all that God accomplishes.

At the very least, contemporary Trinitarian debates have made it clear that just as no one comes to the Father except through the Son and the Spirit, so too, no one comes to the Son except through the events of the scriptural story of salvation. God was present redemptively in those events. This for all Christians is theologically critical. But how are these events to be made real to people living in particular historical and cultural situations? These events themselves must be *mediated* to us in some concrete way. We must be enabled by some *means* to enter into them. The ordinary way this happens, I will argue, is through the activities of worship. For, as we will see in the next chapter, God, who is revealed through the series of redemptive events recounted in Scripture, is also present as those events are performed, preached, or represented in worship. This is the God-appointed way that believers are invited to join in the perichoretic dance of mutuality within God.

This, then, is the final mediation that is necessary for creatures who experience the world fundamentally through their five senses. Human worship always takes on some material and dramatic form. It is necessarily embodied in particular actions that make use of specific objects that worshipers can see, touch, and smell. Further, worship takes shape in spaces that are articulated, for better or worse, to facilitate the movement and actions of the liturgy; it is embodied in melodies and choruses that move worshipers to prayer and praise. All of these objects, expressions, movements, and spaces have visual and sensual contours that have the potential to attract or repel. Thus, any discussion of worship inevitably brings us to the consideration of aesthetics — the ways in which form can spark affections and reflect (or perhaps obstruct), in their turn, the beauty of Christ embodied in the liturgy. Hans Urs von Balthasar has done more than any other theologian to underline the necessity of "form" and therefore of "beauty" in considering the redemptive movement of God in history.

Forms have never played a large role in Protestant discussions of worship, associated as they are with what is "formal" or "impersonal." But von Balthasar insists that the incarnation of God in human and creaturely form makes discussion of form and thus of beauty unavoidable for Christian theology. If beauty in some sense is rooted in God and God's self-communication, as both Edwards and von Balthasar have argued, then art, sometimes in spite of itself, bears some fundamental relation to worship. J. J. von Allmen goes so far as to ask whether art itself is not the longing of all things for liturgical self-expression, the desire "to find their justification in the praise [of God] for which they were created?"[19] So, in calling art into its service, worship not only takes on a form that can potentially speak of God, but also may justify the existence of art itself. We will take up this discussion again at the conclusion of this volume.

In various ways, the following three chapters develop the implications of the Trinitarian character of worship that I have briefly outlined in this chapter. In the following chapter we will think about the *relational* character of worship and of the economic life of the Trinity in particular. In the succeeding chapter we will consider the political dimension of worship that is the form of life appropriate to people

19. von Allmen, *Worship: Its Theology and Practice,* p. 109. On the aesthetics of worship, see Robert P. Glick, *With All Thy Mind: Worship That Honors the Way God Made Us* (Herndon, Va.: Alban Institute, 2006).

formed in Christian worship — the way Christian worship triggers human response. Here we will examine the importance of *agency,* both God's and our own, in worship. Finally, in the concluding chapter, we will reflect on the final mediation of worship in the lives of worshipers, what may be called its *embodiment.* There we will consider the way that worship takes particular material and cultural shape as the aesthetic anticipation of the Christian's life with God in heaven. But the theological framework of this chapter must be kept in mind through all of these reflections. Worship leads us into the life of God. Thinking about the mechanics of worship, as we surely must, should never lead us to think that worship is something under our control. This can all too easily happen. In that case, as Cardinal Godfried Danneels has warned, "The real subject of the liturgy is no longer the Christ, who through the Spirit worships the Father and sanctifies the people in a symbolic act, but the human person or the celebrating community."[20]

SUGGESTIONS FOR FURTHER READING

Christopher Cocksworth. *Holy, Holy, Holy: Worshipping the Trinitarian God.* London: Darton, Longman & Todd, 1997.

William Dyrness. *Visual Faith: Art, Theology, and Worship in Dialogue.* Grand Rapids: Baker, 2001.

Colin Gunton. *The Triune Creator.* Grand Rapids: William B. Eerdmans, 2003.

Belden Lane. "Spirituality as the Performance of Desire: Calvin on the World as a Theatre for the Glory of God." *Spiritus: A Journal of Christian Spirituality* 1, no. 1 (2001): 1-30.

J. J. von Allmen. *Worship: Its Theology and Practice.* New York: Oxford University Press, 1965.

20. Godfried Danneels, "Liturgy Forty Years after the Council," *America,* August 27–September 3, 2007, p. 14.

QUESTIONS FOR DISCUSSION

1. Reflect for a moment on your own tradition of worship (and/or your own worship experience). What persons of the Trinity are emphasized? Why do you think this is the case?

2. Tertullian (one of the church fathers) emphasized that the three persons of the Trinity are experienced in worship "simultaneously" (rather than consecutively). What do you think he meant by this?

3. Recount an experience of worship in which you did become aware of the Trinitarian life of God. How was this accomplished?

4. How can worship practices cultivate the attitude of giving ourselves in obedient response? (Through listening? In silence?) How might this response be a reflection of the Trinity?

CHAPTER 5

The Narrative Shape of Worship

Telling the Story of God's Love

A well-known child's prayer gives voice to a common misconception about God. "I am sorry," the little girl is supposed to have prayed, "that you are stuck way up there in heaven while we are alive down here." While we may not put it in these terms, many people, even Christians, have trouble seeing God as a tangible part of their lives. Perhaps this contributes to a sense that worship is distant and remote from everyday life. The truth, of course, is quite the reverse: God is more present to us than our very breath; he is the concrete one, while we are insubstantial — like a flower that blooms for a while and then fades away. Worship may be one central way in which we as believers can come to terms with both the misconceptions and the reality about God — and ourselves.

In fact, God is present and working in all of history, and in every culture. More particularly, God worked in the events of the life of Christ to bring about salvation. The central events of Christ's life additionally express the dynamic and perichoretic reality of the Trinitarian life of God. As I argued at the end of the last chapter, our access to God is necessarily mediated by these historical events, the actions by which God accomplished and made real the remedy for a sinful and disordered world. What I emphasize in this chapter is the way these actions reflect what we call the economic Trinity, the life of God outside the

95

Godhead. The characteristic of worship to be considered in this chapter is its "relationality." I will argue that at the heart of worship is the celebration of the believer's relationship to God through Christ by the work of the Spirit, as this relationship is mediated through a particular historical narrative. This narrative is constituted by the biblical record of God's creative and redemptive work in Israel and Christ, and the liturgy, in various ways, recounts and represents this narrative. Through the experience of worship, believers enter into the narrative, make it their own, and in this way are formed into the likeness of Christ.

Affirming that worship is effectual is easy enough; making this our actual experience is more difficult. Amid our busy lives, driven by BlackBerries and cell phones, we wonder: How does God show up? And how does this impact the narrative of our lives? Granted that the dramatic narrative of Scripture is the primary means by which we come to know God, we ask ourselves: How do we, citizens of the twenty-first century, have access to these events from hundreds of years ago? How do these theological realities become a part of our lives? Protestants believe that the inspired Scriptures uniquely and authoritatively mediate these events to us today; Catholics would add Episcopal and papal teachings, which normatively interpret the Scriptures and the tradition. But in terms of our personal participation in these events, I will argue that, whatever worship tradition we represent, it is primarily through the special practices of worship that we come to God — and that he approaches us. Our access to God is mediated by the practices of worship — by our prayer, our praise, our hearing of Scripture, and our partaking of the sacraments. In some critical sense, all Christians agree, God is made present to us in these events — even if they do not concur on precisely which practices are necessary and which are optional, or precisely how God is present in this or that practice. For all Christians the practices of worship become carriers of spiritual reality.

Someone will surely ask, But is God *limited* to these practices? Certainly not. God can take the initiative to become known directly through mystical experience, or through dreams or visions. God's people often had such encounters with God in Scripture, and they are not uncommon in the history of the church. But all experiences of this kind are, in one way or another, extraordinary. They do not happen every day, and we are nowhere told to seek them, or to expect them to become regular occurrences. Even in the book of Acts, where these special events are predicted (Acts 2:17-18), it is indicated that it was the regular meeting together for prayer, fellowship, and the apostles' teaching that became normative for believers (see 2:42). God may certainly be revealed through such unusual events, but if we were to depend on such experiences for our faith development, we would risk becoming spiritually undernourished.

It is also true that God is made known through the events of everyday life, through nature and history — what theologians call general revelation. And there is also a sense that our service in the world can, by God's grace, become a carrier of God's presence. But as I will argue in the next chapter, this is true only to the extent that this service and these ordinary experiences of God themselves become an extension, even an embodiment of our prayer and praise — that is, when life itself is understood as part of the narrative of worship. For after all, I will argue, God has ordained particular practices that are enjoined frequently throughout Scripture as the usual ways by which we respond to God's presence in our lives. These practices of worship, which we will examine here, are what we might call the ordinary way to Christian maturity.

Indeed, in this chapter I will develop the argument that God's presence is uniquely made available to believers through the practices of worship. This argument builds on and advances the claim that the Trinity itself provides the basic structure of worship. In the last chapter we moved from a discussion of the internal relations in God to a discussion of the external expression of those eternal relations in redemptive history. Now I will argue that the practices of worship are connected in some special sense to the events of redemptive history. Another way of putting this is to claim that the narrative of worship itself reiterates the narrative of the story of Jesus. The three steps from the immanent Trinity through the economic Trinity to narrative worship are expressed in Figure 1 on page 98.

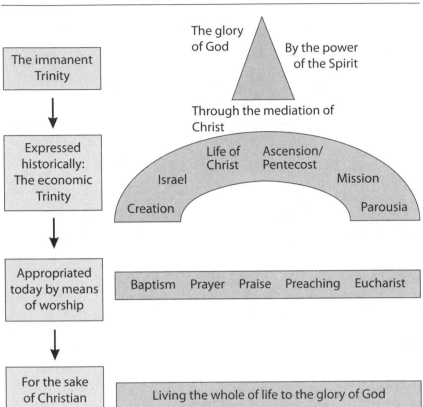

Figure 1. The Threefold Mediation of the Presence of God in Worship

Notice how the table expresses both the twofold movement of worship that we have spoken of and the mediation by which this worship takes place. God comes to us through the events of redemptive history. We appropriate this presence by means of the practices of worship. In turn, these practices, by the working of the Spirit, form us into the likeness of Christ. Calvin liked to talk about the way God accommodates to our understanding. God uses these human activities to speak to us in a language that we can understand. Note that this spiritual process has as its goal our being brought up into the Trinitarian life of God. Again, these same practices, however human they are, have as their end and goal that we actively live our lives before the face of God.

As Calvin said, the goal of the Eucharist is to lift believers into the heavenly places with Christ, to be joined to Christ by the Spirit. But note that this goal of union with Christ is in no way incompatible with the goal that all our lives be lived to the glory of God; indeed, these two realities are two sides of the same coin.

A central concern of the various attempts to renew worship in the twentieth century was the quest to discover ways to connect the experience of worship with the lives of worshipers. As the Second Vatican Council put it, efforts to renew worship should have as their goal to allow for the "full, active, and conscious" participation of everyone in worship. The various worship movements that we reviewed briefly in Chapter Three attempted (or are attempting) in a variety of ways to make this connection, either from the side of contemporary experience, or through a revitalization of traditional worship, or through some combination of these. Some — those on the left of Table 3 in that chapter (p. 70) — are more aggressive about incorporating the contemporary experience of worshipers; others, such as those on the right, are more concerned about re-appropriating the tradition in accessible ways. In that chapter I argued that in each case the resulting combination issues in a particular worship style. Here we will seek to explore how, in a general sense, the practices of worship in their various forms mediate the special presence of God. We will ask, in other words, how our own personal narratives connect with both the narrative of God in history and the narrative of worship. But before doing this, we pause to reflect on the question of what people bring with them — on the narratives that they embrace — when they come into the experience of worship.

The Narratives of Our Lives

For better or worse, worshipers bring their own stories to the experience of worship — stories filled with the hopes and fears of their lives, work, and families. They cannot escape doing this for the important reason that people live out of their stories. Families in many ways are a collection of shared stories, which are told and retold during holiday gatherings. The events of people's lives inevitably contain bits and pieces — illnesses, divorces, failures — that do not seem to fit with the narrative they seek to construct, and so they work to understand these. This lifelong struggle for coherence is one that we all share, and in one way or another it affects our experience of worship. Accordingly, worship leaders and planners must reckon with, and in some way respond to, our personal narratives. We may think of these both in terms of contextual issues, which relate to people's particular histories and culture, and in terms of substantial issues, which relate more universally to what it means to be human.

Contextual Issues

Contextual issues are determined by the cultural formation that people bring with them into worship. This formation inescapably affects what people will expect and hear when they come to worship. Here I will briefly describe three factors that will affect the worshiper in twenty-first-century America. Many others could be mentioned, but these three may be taken as representative factors.

The first contemporary reality is the increasing *pluralism* of our culture. Late modern or what is called postmodern culture is characterized by a diversity of social and cultural worlds that people inhabit and that are interacting in increasingly complex ways. The facts of ethnic and cultural diversity, for example, raise issues that lead to gated communities and reinforced borders on the one hand, and to rich possibilities for intercultural exchange on the other. Then there are issues of religious pluralism that have emerged with particular fierceness in the recent past. These have produced both a fear of radical faith and the terrorism that sometimes accompanies this, but also a renewed respect for people of other faiths. In short, postmodern people can no longer remain content within their cultural or subcultural groupings because they are being thrust into a changing vortex of peoples, values, and faiths. This creates both problems and opportunities to which worship responds.

The second contextual issue is the prominence of economic factors, and often an encroaching *materialism*. Goods and services of all kinds, including services provided by churches, have become increasingly commodified. The result is that every day we are faced with a barrage of advertising images that reflect the multitude of choices we have. Whether we like it or not, or whether we are aware of it or not, we live a large part of our lives as consumers. In this environment, people are socialized to believe that their needs can be met by certain suppliers, and that they as consumers are entitled to satisfaction. If they do not find satisfaction in one place — in one marriage, job, or church — they can always find another that will, in their minds, more nearly meet their needs. As sociologists have pointed out, choosing suppliers is not simply an option but a daily necessity. Often without being aware of it, we make a choice with the assumption that the material advance of the choice will satisfy what are more basic spiritual needs — that, for example, buying this new house will improve our personal and family lives.

Finally, these and other factors have led to an increasingly frantic *pace* of life. It often seems as though burgeoning technical advances and opportunities available to us merely increase the speed of our lives — multiplying as they do the options for entertainment and productivity. We once believed that cell phones and e-mail would make our lives easier; we now fear that we have become captive to their demands. Since we can do more, we have a vague sense that we ought to do more. In the American context at least, these pressures are accompanied by the subtle assumption that our problems surely have some technical or medical solution and that things will (or should) turn out all right in the end.

The mixture of these factors produces a strange combination of escape and denial. We are consumed with the desire to escape and retreat into our own homes — to cocoon ourselves. This reflects a deep and abiding hunger for spiritual nourishment and for a place of peace away from the demands and the drama characteristic of our day. Meanwhile, we deny any signs of weakness or suffering — even, ultimately, signs of death itself — which we hide under a multitude of euphemisms.

These conditions of contemporary life are not evil in themselves, of course. Pluralism and material abundance reflect the diversity and the goodness that God intended for creation; technology and the efficiencies it makes possible are not inherently bad. These can all be stewarded in positive ways. But they do present contemporary believers with particular challenges. We would be naïve not to recognize that economic and political influences in our culture seek to "form" us in particular ways, that amid the events of everyday life there are plenty of conflicting allegiances at work.

Substantial Issues

Of greater importance than the contextual issues are the substantial human concerns that affect our experience of worship.[1] Against the background of these contextual issues, and formed in interaction with them, the narrative we construct or propose for our lives reflects the answers that we give to a series of fundamental questions: Who am I? To whom do I belong? And what do I live for? Notice how all these questions focus on the search for an authentic self. Among educated people in the West, the search for personal fulfillment may be said to have trumped all other human goals. Sociologists have described this search in terms of "expressive individualism." Philosopher Charles Taylor believes this quest assumes that "each one of us has his/her own way of realizing our humanity, and that it is important to find and live out one's own, as against surrendering to conformity with a model imposed on us from outside, by society, or the previous generation, or

1. See the discussion of these in Marva Dawn, *A Royal "Waste" of Time: The Splendor of Worshiping God and Being Church for the World* (Grand Rapids: William B. Eerdmans, 1999), from which these questions are adapted.

religious political authority."[2] Since this searching will obviously shape one's reaction to and participation in worship, let us consider these three questions.

The first of these — Who am I? — reflects the question of our identity. As Robert Schreiter notes in his book *The New Catholicity*, communicators (and, we might add, pastors and worship leaders) are always concerned with the integrity of their message — and, in the case of worship, with the sanctity of their worship tradition.[3] Now this is an issue not only for those with strong church traditions, like the Catholic and the Orthodox, but for anyone who fears change. "The way we have always done things" can be as tough an opponent of change as the strongest liturgical tradition! But worshipers, initially at least, don't care about the integrity of the tradition; they struggle, sometimes painfully, with their own identities. The question that arises, then, is this: How do the practices of worship connect with and nurture worshipers' identities?

A further question that worshipers bring with them is a related query: To whom do I belong? This question is reflected in the contemporary search for roots and the fundamental human need for community. The individualism of American culture is well-known, but what is not always recognized is that Americans, like everyone else, long for community and the sense that they belong to someone or something beyond themselves. Sociologists have debated whether the culture is moving toward increasing isolation or toward identification with a small group of colleagues — whether people today are "bowling alone," as Robert Putnam has argued,[4] or are spending time with "friends" from work. In either case, the longing for security and loyalty is a vital element in the human search for meaning.

Finally, at some point or other, everyone faces this question: What

---

2. Charles Taylor, *A Secular Age* (Cambridge: Harvard University Press/Belknap Press, 2007), p. 475. Taylor argues that this quest for fulfillment is shaped by the Romantic movement of the nineteenth century.

3. Robert Schreiter, *The New Catholicity* (Maryknoll, N.Y.: Orbis Books, 1997).

4. Robert Putnam, "Bowling Alone: America's Declining Social Capital," *Journal of Democracy* 6, no. 1 (January 1995).

103

do I live for? Or, as Charles Taylor puts it, "What is it for which I will literally live or die?" At the end of the day, everyone has in mind some ultimate good, or combination of goods, that he or she pursues in the multiple activities of his or her life. And he or she brings these goals into worship, where they can be either challenged or affirmed.

The Significance of These Issues for Worship

Of course, there will be a variety of responses to the question of the significance these issues have for worship. And there will also be a variety of attitudes toward the significance of people's stories. Some will argue that whatever issues people bring with them to church are ultimately insignificant. What people need to hear is a word from God, and this will simply challenge, and ultimately displace, the human questions and desires that they bring with them. Thinkers with this point of view tend to argue that there is a basic incompatibility between modern culture and the biblical claim of God on our lives. To respond to God, then, means turning our backs on fundamental aspects of our cultural situation. According to these thinkers, worship provides a radically different narrative than the one our culture seeks to construct. On their view, worship is fundamentally counter-cultural.

Others will argue that worship must take these human concerns into account in some way or other, because the goal of the Gospel is the transformation — not the denial — of our cultural and personal narratives. These thinkers believe that the experience of worship encompasses and enlarges the narratives that believers bring to church. They recognize the point that I stressed in the introduction: that worship, among other things, is a particular cultural space, unavoidably related to the surrounding culture but formed by a different story than the one our culture tells. Thus church leaders need to understand and critically appropriate the cultural elements that are used in worship and the way that biblical worship transforms these. The story of the Gospel is different from that of our culture, but this story is not opposed to that one. God's purpose is to redeem creation, not over-throw it. This is the point of view taken in this book. It implies a particular way of reading culture that seeks to learn from it as well as reform it. So culture, as I will argue in the conclusion, can provide important clues that worship may theologically interpret in order to renew itself.

But whichever view toward culture one adopts, it is important to recognize that the role of a congregation's stories, both individual and corporate, is, fundamentally, a theological issue. The question we need to ask is this: What does God think about the narratives of our lives?

The theological issue at stake, I would argue, is whether or not, and in what way, God is already present in the narratives that people are constructing. Does one come to church to find God? Or is God, in some — perhaps inchoate — way, already present in life, calling, nudging one in the direction of faith and a growing awareness of God's presence? The biblical teaching of the universal presence of God's spirit and the universal call of God, however these are understood in detail, would argue for God's presence in people's lives before they come to worship, whether or not they are believers (though of course the way that God deals with believers will be very different from the way he deals with unbelievers). If this is true, and for the present we will assume that it is, we can make this claim: Pastors and leaders should take people's questions into account in considering worship, not for pragmatic reasons (so that the church will grow larger), but for theological reasons. They should take these questions seriously because God has already taken them seriously, and is working in them to lead people to faith or to further Christian maturity.

But how do we know that God takes these questions seriously? Well, arguably, we know this because of the narrative of the Gospel itself. According to this story, God did not wait for people to "figure out" how great he was, but came into history, in Israel and in Christ, to make perfectly clear who he was, and to make possible a new history and a new story, not only for the human race and for creation in general, but also for you and me, for your family and mine in particular. Just as God, in the Old and New Testaments, did not hesitate to enter the narratives of people and nations to disrupt their petty quarrels and projects so that their stories might be re-oriented around a more comprehensive Story — so God is eager to enter our contemporary stories and re-orient them in dramatic ways. The point is that the narrative of God does not efface these little stories — the Gospel is not imperialistic (what postmodern philosophers call "hegemonic"). Rather, this Story encompasses these smaller stories, taking them up into their larger context, filling out the empty spaces and highlighting the gifts and graces that are already present. Worship, then, must engage the narratives of worshipers precisely because the Gospel narrative itself, by the grace of God, since the beginning, was constructed out of such narratives — mysteriously woven together in such a way that, by God's spirit, they became a part of the Kingdom of God.

Worship: God's Narrative and Ours

In the last chapter I argued that the goal of worship is that the worshiper be drawn into the perichoretic life of God. Further, I noted that this incorporation into God's life is accomplished by the historical acts of God — what we call "redemptive history" — because it is that story which uniquely embodies God's promise of salvation. The ultimate importance of these events lies in the fact that there is an eternal connection between them and the Trinitarian life of God — Christ's work, Peter tells us, was established before the foundation of the world (1 Peter 1:20). The narrative of God in history is, in a critical sense, an expression of the life of God itself, and, with the Ascension, this historical narrative in the person of the resurrected Christ has been taken up into that life.

So the life of God bears an eternal connection with the historical events of the life of Christ. We come into the life of God through those historical events — that is, through Christ and by the Holy Spirit. There is no other way. But there is a further portal that is necessary to us. How do we citizens of the twenty-first century come to participate in those historical events? This is where the contemporary practice of worship comes in. The liturgy (that work or practice of the people), as it has developed in the traditions of the church, (re)presents the Story of Christ, and thus expresses both the narrative and the Life this embodies in a form we humans can relate to. In repeatedly coming to God in prayer, reciting the creed, hearing the Bible read and preached, and taking the elements of communion, God's people are progressively being transformed into what Paul calls the likeness of Jesus Christ. In hearing the story again and again, believers begin to become the story. But notice how the theological meaning occurs in and through the practice, over time, of the actions of worship. This meaning takes shape through both the juxtaposition and the flow of the words and the actions.

One way of thinking about the narrative of worship is to liken it to a melody. A familiar melody carries us along without thinking, even as it affects us at the deepest levels of our being. We find ourselves humming a familiar melody at various points in our day; together we sing songs that remind us of significant events in our lives. It is a commonplace that music often serves to structure our personal and communal experience. Similarly, the narrative of worship is structured with a kind of musical logic. We are carried along by its movement, and we respond at a deep level to its juxtapositions and resolutions. The goal of worship is to connect the melody of worship with the (often discordant) melodies of our lives, and, by the grace of God, to achieve a harmony between and among these various melodies. Now we will look at the constituent parts of this melody of worship, speaking of this flow in the four basic elements that constitute worship — however wide the variety of styles that may express these elements.

The Gathering

Worship begins with God in the sense that God authors our lives and has, in Jesus Christ, provided salvation from all that has disrupted our lives. Further, God has taken the initiative in the biblical narrative to call people to come, or return, to him. God calls Abraham to leave his home and country and be the father of many; God calls Israel out of Egypt, into the land of promise, and back from the bondage of the Exile; Jesus calls Peter to leave his nets and follow him, and Paul to become his ambassador; and so on. Similarly, God calls each of us. This call, then, is the beginning of our worship. God reiterates this same call each Sunday as the pastor or priest says, "The LORD is king! Let the earth rejoice!" (Ps. 97:1) or "The mighty one, God the LORD, speaks and summons the earth from the rising of the sun to its setting" (Ps. 50:1). We are invited to join the great company of believers, from all times and places, who have heard and responded to the call of God. Today, whatever the circumstances of our lives, whatever the trials we may be experiencing, God invites us to worship.

There are several ways in which the opening of worship can articulate this active process of being gathered out of the world for worship. Usually there is a formal call to worship of some kind. The pastor might say, "Come, let us worship." Then follows a prayer and perhaps a hymn of adoration. In these ways the congregation is invited to praise the God who calls them together. The focus is on God's greatness, goodness, and love.

In certain worship traditions, a statement of confession and pardon is placed early in the service, as an aspect of the gathering. This is one way in which the rich medieval penitential tradition is continued in contemporary worship. This statement expresses the fact that humans have gone astray and proven themselves unworthy of worshiping a holy God. Of course, by our baptism we are washed and forgiven, in and through the death of Christ, but we acknowledge week by week that we continue to fall short of God's glory and are in constant need of forgiveness. We live, as Martin Luther put it, by the forgiveness of our sins. Whether this acknowledgment is made in a formal prayer or a simple statement by the pastor, the awareness of our status as forgiven sinners is, in most Protestant worship, a critical component of the time we spend in God's presence.

Again, in some styles of worship, the practice of "passing the peace" follows the statement by the pastor that "in Jesus Christ we are forgiven." After the confession and pardon, people are invited to greet those sitting around them. Having been reminded of the forgiveness that is ours in Christ, believers are invited to enjoy the communion this forgiveness inevitably creates. In the Gospels, the connection between forgiveness and community is especially emphasized. In fact, Matthew goes so far as to say that if your brother or sister holds something against you, you should leave your gift at the altar and make it right before returning to worship (Matt. 5:23-24). This implies that worship cannot be truly complete as long as forgiveness is not manifest (practiced) in the community.

The Service of the Word of God

After believers are invited and gathered (and thus forgiven) by God, worship can proceed through the reading and proclaiming of God's Word. In the Reformed tradition, this constitutes the central focus of worship. According to this tradition, God is specially present in the proclaimed Word. In the gathering we recall that we are lost but that God has found us in Jesus Christ; in the Word we remember that we are confused and in need of guidance, and this is provided in God's Word. The Word of God provides instruction for believers that goes beyond their natural (and often self-serving) wisdom. When the congregation hears the lector repeat "This is the Word of God," they are reminded that this instruction is something that, spiritually, they cannot do without. The Word comprehends the teaching of creation in the Wisdom literature, the expression of God's will for us in the law, and the necessary correction of our errant ways in the teaching of the prophets, and of Christ and the apostles.

This aspect of the service is also shaped in various ways in Christian traditions. Often there will be special prayers that ask God to illumine minds and prepare hearts to "hear" what is being read and preached. Then there are formal "readings" of Scripture, perhaps from the Old and New Testaments, and often from the Psalms. The public reading of Scripture is an ancient tradition of the church that goes back to the time before the parts of the New Testament were formally collected — when letters or parts of the Gospels were read to the assembled congregation. This practice has great symbolic and practical significance. We are seated under the Word; we listen and reflect on what we hear. In some traditions the Gospel lesson is read in the middle of the standing congregation, symbolizing the coming of God in the midst of his people in Jesus Christ.

The sermon or homily is the opportunity for the pastor, in the corporate and contemporary context, to reflect on the Scripture that was read. On behalf of the people, the leader expands on the reading and suggests ways in which it might apply to their lives — thus implying the larger context of worship in everyday life. The substance of sermons is determined by the worship style that is embodied in a given congregation. The revival style would tend to orient sermons toward making a decision; those in the style of Christian nurture would focus more on the spiritual nurture of the congregation; and so on. These same factors would also determine whether and in what way the pastor would call for some response after the sermon — whether the pastor would call congregants to come to the altar or to spend some time in quiet reflection on the theme of the sermon.

Often this part of the service will include the creed and other prayers that will focus on the needs of the people in the light of what has been preached and heard. In creedal churches, recitation of a creed or confession, week by week, reminds the congregation of its core beliefs — those things for which God calls them to live or die. Reciting the creed is more than a pedagogical device; it is a performative act. In an important sense, it realizes what it speaks about. By speaking our faith, we become believers. The corporate nature of both the creed and public prayers is an important reminder that the practices of worship are, first of all, for the sake of the community — they are communal. In corporate worship, individual nurture and growth are certainly in view, but always within the larger perspective of the whole people of God. In Paul's great statement of the goal of the Christian life in Ephesians, he underlines this corporate context: The gifts used in worship are given, he says, "to equip the saints for the work of ministry, for building up the body of Christ, until all of us come to the unity of the faith and of the knowledge of the Son of God, to maturity, to the measure of the full stature of Christ" (Eph. 4:12-13).

The Eucharist or Communion

The Eucharist or, literally, the offering of thanksgiving, follows the preaching of the Word and is often connected to it in various ways (by the sermon, the reading of Scripture, or some other way). Its centerpiece is the table of the Lord, where God feeds his people with the heavenly food of the sacrament. This part of worship resonates at several points with the narrative of God in Scripture. God fed the people of Israel in the wilderness until they entered the Promised Land; Israel offered her firstfruits to the Lord and celebrated these gifts with a festival; Jesus fed the multitudes in the Gospels and established this sacrament at his last supper with his disciples. There in the words of institution, as recorded by Paul, Jesus gathered up all the "feeding narratives" of Scripture by offering his own body as the nourishment for his disciples: "This is my body that is for you. Do this in remembrance of me" (1 Cor. 11:24).

It is unfortunate that these words have become such a battleground in the history of the church, because the basic underlying meaning of Christ's statement is clear. In Christ's body and blood — that is, through his death and resurrection — we are given Christ's saving presence to the end of time. These elements, however understood, thus stand in place of this presence; they recall it and in some mysterious way they represent it. There is a sense, then, that Christ is *really present* among his people in this practice, however this might be comprehended in detail. Because of this presence, the Christian gives thanks and makes her offering (which is usually taken just before, or sometimes after, the communion), in token of the giving of herself in response to Christ's self-giving.

Various actions accompany the celebration of this feast and add to the drama and meaning. The offering is taken, as we noted, usually just before communion, while the elements are being prepared. This juxtaposition underlines the connection between the self-giving of God in Christ and our response. Indeed, these events highlight in a striking way the mutual self-giving that echoes the life of God. I still recall the time this was first brought home to me. While visiting an Episcopal church (which is not my tradition) years ago, I was struck by the fact that while ushers were taking our gifts and laying them on the altar, the priests were, *at the same time,* preparing the elements for the communion that was to follow. My response was to wonder, *What's happening here? Who is giving what to whom?* Well, God is being given to us in the body of Christ, and we are responding by giving ourselves to God. Worship at that moment had become a commotion of mutual self-giving, in which both directions of worship — from God to us and from us to God — are celebrated at the same time.

The invitation to the table usually follows the offering, expressing, on behalf of God, the divine hospitality for those who come in faith. In some traditions the sacrament of baptism is performed at this point in the service, to signify our obedient response to God's gracious invitation presented in the Word that was preached. Seeing people come to receive baptism, or seeing parents bring their children, serves to remind the gathered community of their own baptism and the cleansing and renewal that this represents. It continues to signify that, by baptism, we have been made participants in Christ's death and resurrection.

In the transition to the service of communion, the pastor (or an elder) offers the thanksgiving and blessing, breaks the bread, and distributes the bread and wine — all significant echoes of the biblical narratives of feeding and blessing. Just as God's people were fed with manna in the wilderness, so we are given God's provision for our spiritual needs, and, in anticipation of the heavenly banquet of God with his people, we are given present nourishment for our corporate lives. The passing and sharing of the elements reiterates the mutual sharing of God's people, and becomes a visible sign of the mutual sharing that characterizes the perichoretic dance of the Trinity.

Our stress on practices risks giving the impression that all four of these parts of the liturgy carry equal weight. But reflection on the underlying narrative that these events are meant to signal reminds us that this narrative has a center — the life, death, and resurrection and ascension of Christ. Since the narrative rests on this fulcrum, it follows that the practice which presents this is, in some way, unique. This uniqueness leads theologian Miroslav Volf to say that the Eucharist and baptism, what the church calls sacraments, belong in a category separate from the other practices.[5] This biblical and theological centrality is often signaled by their placement in the service, but it is still carried by the ordered practices of worship.

The Sending

God not only calls us and, by means of the Word, teaches us and feeds us; God also sends us back into the world. Thus the practices that bring the service to an end have significance beyond the mere closing of the time of worship. They are themselves theologically important in concluding the narrative of calling and sending that characterizes the biblical story. The notion of sending implies the particular call of God to "go into all the world and proclaim the good news" (Mark 16:15). But there is also a strong ethical component in God's sending: we are now to be the people of God in the world. Jesus put it this way in the Sermon on the Mount: "Let your light shine before others, so that they may see your good works and give glory to your Father in heaven" (Matt. 5:16). This ethical and missionary calling implies God's intention to draw people to respond to the Good News, and eventually to come and join in worship. The relationship between worship and mission is described in Figure 2 on page 114.

This portion of the service may include a hymn that focuses on the life that God wants believers to live in the world. It may include a

5. Volf argues that Christian beliefs are "normatively inscribed in sacraments" in a way they are not in other practices, and hence they "ritually enact normative patterns for practices." In *Practicing Theology,* ed. Miroslav Volf and Dorothy Bass, quoted in Simon Chan, *Liturgical Theology: The Church as Worshiping Community* (Downers Grove, Ill.: InterVarsity Press, 2007), p. 182n.20.

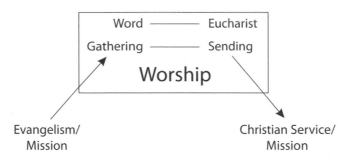

Figure 2

prayer of dedication, and it always includes a benediction, a special blessing on the congregation as they go. Often this is a biblical benediction such as the Aaronic blessing from Numbers 6:24-26: "The LORD bless you and keep you; the LORD make his face to shine upon you, and be gracious to you; the LORD lift up his countenance upon you, and give you peace." Clearly, if the service simply ends with a casual "See you next week!", the narrative of God's presence is left unfinished. Just as children in the Old Testament period did not want to leave their parents' home without a blessing, so we, who are God's children, need this blessing today.

Conclusion: On the Form of Worship

These practices shape us week by week into the people of God and into the likeness of Christ, by the Spirit. As with all practices, there is a period of learning and repetition, and, inevitably, there will be the development of habits. Habits, of course, can become dreary and tiresome (remember the warnings we reflected on in Chapter Three), but they can also be healthy and life-giving. Worship, like eating and sleeping, is a practice that is essential not only to spiritual growth but also to our development as human beings.

The story that shapes worship includes the assertion that human beings are created in the image of God, created to respond to and, ultimately, to worship the Creator. The end for which humans are made includes centrally the call to respond to God in prayer, praise, and thanksgiving. The Christian story contends that we are most fully human when we stand in the presence of God and give thanks.

But humans are also flesh-and-blood creatures who live in a world of cell phones and sunsets. They cannot survive long in the mystical heights that we sometimes associate with worship. So worship, to be accessible to creatures like us, must undergo a final mediation. It must be translated into particular forms and shapes — it needs to be embodied in acts like kneeling and bowing, or in objects like the cross and images of the Virgin. This means that worship has, inevitably, as we have pointed out, an aesthetic and a tactile dimension. Whether we think about it or not, the movement of the liturgy shapes and is shaped by imagination. The relationship between worship and imagination needs far more attention than we — at least on the Protestant side of things — tend to give it. We have stressed that the practices of worship embody a narrative or a melody of love and mutual self-giving that ultimately reflects the being of God. Our worship implies that at the center of things stands a personal being who reflects these characteristics. If we see the world in these terms, we will surely see the objects and events of our lives against a much larger canvas than we would if we saw the world as autonomous and self-contained. We will be led to see our own search for human fulfillment in a different and more comprehensive light.

When we call people to God in our missions and evangelism, we are calling them to a particular way of imagining the world, and therefore to a particular aesthetic. This is a critical if often overlooked aspect of our worship, and we will give it extensive attention in the final chapter. One way of elaborating this imaginative construal of life is to consider our life with God as a drama. We have spoken of worship as a response to what God has done and is doing in the world. Theologians Kevin Vanhoozer and Hans Urs von Balthasar have proposed that we think of Christian faith in terms of a theodrama. The understanding that we seek in developing our faith is not simply a cognitive understanding but a theodramatic understanding — that is, an understanding in terms of what our dramatic part will be in the play of which God is the director.

As noted in the introductory chapter, worship puts us into play and lays claim to our lives, because in worship we are not spectators but actors in the play. We are on the stage and called to say our part and make our special impact. Scripture, then, can be seen as a kind of sacred script, and discipleship can be thought of in terms of the category of performance. For our purposes here, this conception is especially helpful in connecting the narrative of our lives with the narrative of worship that I have described in this chapter. Seen from the perspective of theodrama, these narratives are both part of the larger play that God is directing. Worship in the sense in which we are developing it here has a particular dramatic shape. It becomes a local performance that echoes that larger drama of salvation history and that we in turn are called to perform in our own setting. There is a dramatic scarlet thread of God's saving work in history that connects these scenes of the theodrama.[6]

AT THE END of the day, worship has a single role to play in the lives of believers: to retell, re-present, and thus refresh the story of God's love and call. The great dramatic climax pictured in Revelation is the scene in which people of every tongue and nation bow down before the Lamb that was slain (Rev. 7:9). Everything in worship is subordinated to this end and leads to this goal. Similarly, everything we do in worship, our prayers, and our response in faith and devotion has a single goal: to allow us to indwell this story and make it our own. In other words, these practices are effective when they encourage and sustain the relationships with God, creation, and each other that the Gospel makes possible. Likewise, we, nourished and renewed by the narrative of worship, have a single calling: to tell and live out this great story, to remind ourselves and those around us again and again that God was in Christ reconciling the world to himself. We will explore this calling further in the following chapter, where we will consider the agency that worship encourages.

6. See Kevin Vanhoozer, *The Drama of Doctrine: A Canonical-Linguistic Approach to Christian Theology* (Louisville: Westminster John Knox, 2005); and Hans Urs von Balthasar, *Theo-Drama: Theological Dramatic Theory,* trans. Graham Harrison (San Francisco: Ignatius Press, 1988).

Earlier I argued that worship, when it is effective, has a distinct melody line that forms worshipers over time. I also alluded to the fact that individual worshipers are brought into a larger community of believers so that their stories become part of this communal story. These stories in turn are taken up into the movement of the liturgy week by week. One might argue that God's purpose is to see the melodies of these stories blend together in a kind of polyphony, where the Gospel promise and the Trinitarian love of God provide the basic melody line. Here God is seen not only as the lover who seeks us out, or the teacher who instructs us, but as the composer who crafts a larger symphony out of the various thematic elements that comprise our human communities. We might then see worship as a kind of rehearsal for the people of every tongue and nation, who will endlessly sing the praises of God around the throne, singing, as John says, "Salvation belongs to our God who is seated on the throne, and to the Lamb!" (Rev. 7:10).

There is an old baptismal formula that was used among the Huguenot believers in the sixteenth and seventeenth centuries when they baptized their children that captures the basic melody line beautifully. As the pastor holds the child, before sprinkling the water of baptism, he repeats,

> For you, baby Maria, God made the world out of nothing.
> For you, baby Maria, God called Israel out of Egypt.
> And for you, baby Maria, God brought Israel back from Exile.
> For you, baby Maria, Christ came into the world to teach
>   the children.
> For you, baby Maria, Christ died on the cross and rose again.
> For you, baby Maria, God sent the Holy Spirit to give you strength
>   to live as you ought.
> For you, baby Maria, Christ will come again and take us to God.
> Baby Maria, you know nothing of this.
> But we promise to tell you the story until you make it your own.
> And so I baptize you in the name of the Father, the Son,
>   and the Holy Spirit. . . .

SUGGESTIONS FOR FURTHER READING

Marva Dawn. *A Royal "Waste" of Time: The Splendor of Worshiping God and Being Church for the World*. Grand Rapids: William B. Eerdmans, 1999.

Marlea Gilbert et al. *The Work of the People: What We Do in Worship and Why*. Herndon, Va.: Alban Institute, 2007.

Robert Schreiter. *The New Catholicity*. Maryknoll, N.Y.: Orbis Books, 1997.

Charles Taylor. *A Secular Age*. Cambridge: Harvard University Press/ Belknap Press, 2007.

Leanne Van Dyk, ed. *A More Profound Alleluia: Theology and Worship in Harmony*. Grand Rapids: William B. Eerdmans, 2005.

Kevin Vanhoozer. *The Drama of Doctrine: A Canonical-Linguistic Approach to Christian Theology*. Louisville: Westminster John Knox, 2005.

QUESTIONS FOR DISCUSSION

1. Explain some of the reasons why we worry about being overly conformed to the world. Are these reasons always legitimate? Why or why not?

2. What is the value (or danger) involved in saying that the stories of people are theologically significant?

3. Take elements of worship and talk about how these practices shape us — for example, the offering, the passing of the peace, confession, and so on.

4. How do you think the narrative of worship relates to the traditions of spirituality that we spoke about in Chapter Three? Another way of posing this question is to ask whether there is only one narrative of worship, or are there many?

5. What are the limitations of talking about worship in terms of narrative? Or in terms of a melody? What other model or models might be suggested?

CHAPTER 6

The Lessons of Worship

Practicing What We Believe

I have argued that worship leads believers to tell and live out the story of God's love in Jesus Christ. Worship, in other words, is transformative. And in order to bring about this renewal, worship needs to work faith down into the emotions and reflexes of believers, making them responsive to God in the whole of life. That is, worship, though grounded in something that God has done and continues to do in the world, reaches its goal in moving worshipers to be active participants in what God is doing. Worship is about making believers into the agents of God's dramatic purposes in the world. Worship, when it is vital, stimulates the agency of God's people.

This seems fairly straightforward and noncontroversial. But the devil — or in this case, God — is in the details. How precisely does this happen? How can worship contribute to this living out of the Gospel? How does worship move us to do different sorts of things? The answer theologically is that it does this by shaping us into the image of Christ, by the Spirit. But that too seems a bit vague. So in this chapter, we ask, What kind of people are shaped in this way? What would they look like if you ran into them on the street?

What does someone formed by Christian worship look like? One can hardly think of a more important question for Christians at the beginning of the twenty-first century — in our pluralistic, materialistic, driven, post-secular world; and in a Christian world beset by quarrels over the very meaning of worship. The argument that I will attempt to make in this chapter is that the identity of Christians grows out of worship, because the practices of worship shape them into a particular polity, or way of living together. This is a chapter, in other words, on worship and politics. The initial reaction to this connection may be a negative one. Trying to relate worship and politics is certainly obscure, you will say, and probably perverse. When you come to church, you want to *escape* from politics. Indeed, for most people worship is a kind of escape from the difficulties of real life, including politics. It is a place of retreat where one can heal bruised sensibilities and build up spiritual resources in order to re-engage the world. Politics, on the other hand, implies a dog-eat-dog mentality that seems the furthest thing possible from the quiet intimacy we long for in worship.

There is certainly truth in all this. Worship should be a place of healing; it should include quiet places for meditation and prayer; and yes, it should allow us to build up our spiritual resources. But this raises again the question of what these resources look like. What shape do they take? Here is where, inescapably, the polity of the Christian life comes in. Politics, in general terms — and the way we will use it here — is the just ordering of human lives and relationships. Thus the politics implied in worship expresses, among other things, the kind of people God intended us to be — the way we are to relate to one another, in Christ, by the Spirit. The claim I want to advance here is that there is a particular set of habits, a polity, embedded in the practices of worship.

The Polity of the Christian Life: What Orders Our Life Together?

There is a long-standing debate within the Christian family about the relationship between the polity we are talking about and worship. Some Christians from the Anabaptist tradition are quite convinced that the shaping that goes on in worship is so extraordinary — indeed, so miraculous — that it produces people whose polity is inscrutable to those outside the church. This means that there can be no (direct) application of this Christian way of living together to, say, the running of government or business. Worship produces people who indwell what these Christians call a radical counterculture that witnesses to the broader culture precisely by its difference. Other Christians from a more Reformed perspective would prefer to say that worship shapes believers in a way that restores their created dignity and therefore, inevitably, has a broader application to our lives in the world. People from this perspective would say that, in an important sense, every human pursuit has something to learn from the practices of worship.

It is not my purpose here to settle this debate, or to argue for one side or the other — though my own Reformed perspective will undoubtedly show through. Rather, what I want to do here is highlight the importance of the historical and cultural context in which worship is carried out. The church goes through historical periods in which its polity is clearly distinguishable from that of the world around it — as it was, for example, during the first centuries. The church also goes through periods in which its patterns are reflected in the larger culture, as happened after the conversion of Constantine in C.E. 312. The relations between church polity and public polity, in other words, are as often a reflection of historical and cultural factors as they are of any particular theological standpoint. One might venture to say that in the early centuries, the church's challenge was to *develop the consequences of its polity* more clearly; and during the Constantinian period, the need was rather to *differentiate its special polity* more clearly from that of the world around it. In cases like the former, the danger is that the church will appear irrelevant to the larger culture. In cases like the latter, the danger is that its polity will be co-opted and thus distorted by that culture.

If these broad characterizations have any truth, then one might contend further that the challenge facing the church at the beginning of this new century is more like the second than the first of these examples. Although I cannot argue the case here, there is growing evidence that the way of life of most Christians in America today is indistinguishable from that of their neighbors.[1] For that reason, our emphasis in this chapter will be on the ways in which the polity of worship ought to be distinguished from that of the world around it. What actual difference *should* worship make in the life of believers?

Already in the New Testament, believers were concerned about the difference Christian worship practices should make. This is understandable, because in the first generations of the church, Christians made up a tiny minority in the great Roman Empire. They had therefore to understand precisely how their polity differed from that of the larger and in every way much more powerful world around them. Paul is surely thinking of this relationship when he writes in his letter to the Philippians,

> Only, live your life in a manner worthy of the gospel of Christ, so that, whether I come and see you or am absent and hear about you, I will know that you are standing firm in one spirit, striving side by side with one mind for the faith of the gospel. (1:27)

Apparently the Philippians were very proud of being "Roman citizens," citizens of the most powerful empire the world had ever known. (This at least is the way they would have characterized themselves.) Paul was concerned to explain to them the new ways they needed to learn to live together, the new polity implied in the Gospel, and especially the ways this differed from the politics of the empire so evident around them. In the third chapter of this letter to them, he goes on to distinguish this way of living from that of those whose "minds are set on earthly things" (3:19). In contrast, Paul emphasizes, "our citizenship [Gr. *politeia*] is in heaven, and it is from there that we are expecting a Savior, the Lord Jesus Christ. He will transform the body of our humiliation that it may be conformed to the body of his glory, by the power that also enables him to make all things subject to himself. Therefore, my brothers and sisters, whom I love and long for, my joy and crown, stand firm in the Lord in this way, my beloved" (3:20-21; 4:1).

---

1. See the argument in Ron Sider, *The Scandal of the Evangelical Conscience* (Grand Rapids: Baker, 2005).

Notice how the norms that Paul speaks about are to be shaped by the story that we have entered by our baptism and that we replicate in worship. Reference to our baptism reminds us that the practices of worship do not translate into public behavior on a one-to-one basis. Baptism and the Lord's Supper, for example, do not sanctify our hygienic and dining practices (though they may change the way we think about them). These sacraments are unique, divinely appointed events that symbolize deep theological truths about our relationship with God. But I want to argue that these and other worship practices can develop sensitivities that impact our corporate and public lives. Their performance over time develops habits that are reflected in our everyday lives. What we pray for is that our family and community patterns resonate with the patterns of worship.

The patterns of worship should shape our lives because they articulate something essential about the new humanity we have been given in Christ. But Paul implies a further reason for their importance: they enact what we will one day become when Christ returns. Our citizenship is both in this world and its culture and, Paul insists, in heaven, from whence we await a savior. This is the point at which our understanding of eschatology (literally, "the study of last things") connects with the practices of worship.

Traditionally, eschatology focused primarily on what are called end-time events: the return of Christ, the Last Judgment, and so on. But in the last generation scholars have begun to place more emphasis on our present experience of Christ's resurrection and the gifts of the Holy Spirit. Whereas previously more emphasis was placed on those parts of God's future that believers had "not yet" experienced, now there is more prominence given to what we "already" have in Christ. And the practices of worship can represent those aspects of God's promised future that, because of the pouring out of the Holy Spirit, we can already enjoy in the present.

Notice how Paul's description of our "polity" stresses the hope of Christians, when Christ returns and completes the transformation that is begun with our baptism. In an important sense, because of the comprehensive story of worship, our lives are controlled not only by the past but also by the future. For the future of Christians might be described as an infinitely enriched experience of worship — something I will comment on in the conclusion of this volume. But in a more general sense, every human institution is controlled by its future. As philosopher James K. A. Smith has argued, the norms of a particular community are always determined by the goal of that community, which in turn is unfolded in the story this community tells about itself.[2]

It is sometimes argued that too much emphasis on the future, when Christ returns to establish his kingdom, will undermine the motivation to act in this present order. But if God's future is understood properly, nothing could be further from the truth. The vision of what God is going to do actually *inspires* our present behavior. In a sense, this is true of human projects as well. Consider the norms of a football or soccer team. Its life together is governed by the goal of the formation of that team: to bring glory to a particular city (or country) by winning a championship — or at least having a winning season. In an important sense, everything that team does is controlled by this (future) goal. This objective disciplines everything about the team as a unit: its rules for travel, its pre-game meals, its curfews, its practice, and its relationships with outsiders. This shapes the story it tells about itself. Nothing is allowed to distract the members of the team from focusing on this aspiration. The goal of a championship thus determines the polity of that group.

One might say something similar about the polity of Christians. The goal of our heavenly communion with the Triune God determines the polity of our earthly Christian community, and, I would argue, the practices of worship are what teach us about this alternative polity. Worship by its very nature witnesses to the impermanence of this world and its goal in the New Heaven and the New Earth. In projecting an alternative future to the one that governments promise, the practices of worship are political acts. Reformed theologian J. J. von

2. James K. A. Smith, *Introducing Radical Orthodoxy* (Grand Rapids: Baker, 2004), pp. 201-3.

Allmen notes, "To say 'glory be to God' is to protest against the powers and the powerful who imagine that they can fulfill the longings of humanity."[3] The liturgy, then, is political because it forms us in ways alternative to those of our national political culture — though, as I have argued, not in ways *opposed* to that culture. It is the place where the patterns of the kingdom life are practiced and appropriate habits are formed. So in this chapter we want to ask, What polity is implied by the practices of worship? What follows are five possible ways to answer this question.

The Lessons of the Liturgy

The Liturgy Teaches Hospitality

At the beginning of worship, the leader stands and announces, "Come, let us worship God" (or some variant of this). In this call to worship there is implicit an amazing claim: that God invites everyone, whatever his or her background or situation, to come into his presence and worship. In Scripture this invitation takes many forms, as we have seen, from the call of Abraham, to the call of Israel, to the "return" to God during the Exile, to the prodigal son returning to the waiting father (in Luke 15). What makes this political is that, in the case of worship, this invitation is extended by a *human* community on behalf of God. Since God has reconciled us to himself, Paul says, he has committed to *us* the ministry of reconciliation. Since we have shared in the event of being reconciled to God in Christ, we have necessarily become bearers of the news of that event. Here is how Paul puts it:

> All this is from God, who reconciled us to himself through Christ, and has given us the ministry of reconciliation; that is, in Christ God was reconciling the world to himself, not counting their tres-

3. J. J. von Allmen, *Worship: Its Theology and Practice* (New York: Oxford University Press, 1965), p. 64. See also p. 57.

passes against them, and entrusting the message of reconciliation to us. (2 Cor. 5:18-19)

The call to worship, then, the open doors of the church, imply that this congregation, echoing God's own welcome, has an attitude of openness to anyone and everyone who might wish to join this activity, whatever their spiritual condition.

Like everyone else, I often see signs on the announcement boards of churches I pass indicating the time of the Sunday morning worship, frequently followed by a little notice: "All are welcome." I admit that I often think to myself, *Yeah — right! I'm sure they wouldn't welcome me, or maybe someone who looked different than they do.* It is true, these familiar invitations notwithstanding, that Christians do not always live up to this declaration; the history of the church is filled with examples where Christians engage in practices that exclude rather than welcome. But to recall this sad history is to miss the point that this familiar invitation expresses. While this group may not be as welcoming as they should, they belong to a community that is *supposed to* welcome outsiders. This is what this congregation believes about itself because *this is what it believes about God.* Thus the congregation's calling, in part, is to be a people who reflect God and welcome strangers. The sign in front of their building indicates that they know this, whatever their actual practice may be. They come together week by week and put this sign outside their sanctuary so that, little by little, they might — please God — become the kind of people who welcome everyone who comes.

It is a sociological fact that people prefer to be with friends and families rather than strangers. It is also a fact that churches are, for the most part, made up of people of a similar background. Despite all the talk about multiculturalism and multicultural churches, actual examples of working congregations of mixed backgrounds, though increasing, are still somewhat rare. But again, these facts miss the vital point of the Christian polity. In spite of ourselves, and even in spite of frequent failings in this respect, the Christian church still announces to the world the fact that God is open to all who want to come, and that a people formed in the polity of Christian worship will be a welcoming and, ultimately, a diverse people. The practices of worship nurture in people a spirit of welcome, and they seek, by God's grace, and in spite of many failed attempts, to overcome their parochialism and become welcoming to the stranger and the foreigner. Thus the church's polity stands as a silent but powerful rebuttal to the sociological law that people will *always* prefer to be with their own kind, because this is a community whose core values include openness and hospitality.

The Liturgy Teaches Reconciliation and Love

The practice of openness to outsiders is closely linked to a second aspect of the polity of worship. At the center of worship is the celebration of Christ's sacrifice on the cross in which, Paul says in 2 Corinthians 5:19, God was reconciling the world to himself. The realization that God, by our faith and baptism, has brought about a situation in which we, in spite of our failings, are reconciled to God is something that leads us to worship — it elicits our praise and prayer. The act of representing this event is characteristically called the Eucharist or thanksgiving.

Again, this practice of worship implies a certain polity. At the heart of the polity of worship is the claim that despite differences, prejudice, and suspicions, we can be reconciled not only to God but also with each other. Reconciliation is ultimately God's work; it is a miracle. We cannot by ourselves reconcile people either to God or to their neighbor. Only God through the work of Christ can bring us into the loving mutuality that characterizes the Trinity. But this theological reality of reconciliation leads us to a particular way of being in the world and gives us a special sensitivity toward human relationships. Christians formed by this polity are called to be a conciliatory people. Bearing in themselves the reality of being reconciled to God, Christians can even become agents of reconciliation. As Paul puts it, "So we are ambassadors for Christ, since God is making his appeal through us; we entreat you on behalf of Christ, be reconciled to God" (2 Cor. 5:20).

In many worship services, the call to worship is followed by a shared confession in which the congregation together remembers their failings and asks God in Christ to forgive. This practice reminds those who gather week by week that they are a people who need to be forgiven, not once for all but again and again. They do not claim any special exemption from sin and selfishness, but rather, amazingly, recognize exactly the kind of people they are. But this practice also reminds them that, in Christ, there is forgiveness. Christians believe that sin can be overcome and relationships restored and attitudes healed. By the practice of confession, they are, in other words, being prepared to receive the gift of Christ's body and blood in the Eucharist.

In the style of worship most familiar to me, the confession and pardon are followed immediately by the passing of the peace. This is the time that everyone is to turn to those nearby and greet them — and perhaps do something like my daughter did when she was younger: take the opportunity to run to the other side of church and invite her friend to spend the night on Friday. Again, I have to admit that my initial reaction to this part of the service is much like my reaction to the "All are welcome" sign outside the church. A part of me says, *What hypocrisy! Why should I greet these people who I don't know and who probably aren't interested in greeting me?* But each time I stretch out my hand to a stranger or hug a friend, something happens. I am reminded by the practice of the polity of this community that this is the kind of people we *are becoming* in Christ. Whether I feel like meeting someone or not is irrelevant. Our life in Christ has this particular conciliatory shape to it. As a result, this is a community in which sharing and conciliation are core values, and, by the practices of worship, these values are being formed in me.

I have seen a pastor reach his hands down into the baptismal font and let the water run from his hands as he recited the words of forgiveness: "In Christ we are forgiven." There in graphic form is the connection between our forgiveness and the baptism on which it is based, reminding us that this confession is possible because of our baptism and the new resurrection life that we find there. True enough, we often come to church tired out after a busy week, bearing grudges against this or that co-worker or family member, or distracted by an array of concerns. Repeating the confession and shaking our neighbor's hand do not magically make us into loving and forgiving people. But these actions remind us, week by week, that we are *supposed to be* forgiving people. Moreover, these actions teach us that by the grace of Christ and the power of the Spirit, we are becoming this kind of people. It is not hard to see how unique this practice is. Where else in our culture do we go around shaking hands with strangers and admitting out loud (in front of them) our mistakes?

The Liturgy Allows Us to Lament

Worship includes spaces for another kind of practice that shapes our lives together: the lament. In Scripture this is a literary genre evident in certain psalms. In Psalm 22, for example, in probably the most well-known lament (the words that Christ later spoke from the cross), the psalmist cries out, "My God, my God, why have you forsaken me? Why are you so far from helping me?" (Ps. 22:1). Laments were songs that allowed Israel to express (to God) her deepest sorrows and fears, all focusing centrally on the sense of being forsaken by God. This was an important aspect of the Hebrews' worship, a part of their corporate prayer life.

Lament may seem like a strange thing to bring into our worship. Worship is supposed to strengthen and heal, so why should we spend time expressing our sorrow or grieving over some loss or misfortune? Is complaining to God an appropriate activity for worship? The truth is, of course, that we don't spend any time doing this in most worship services today — and we do it even less in the larger culture, characterized as it is by euphemism and denial. In fact, theologians Kathleen Billman and Daniel Migliore did a study of many modern liturgies and found that the psalms of lament were consistently omitted in the corporate reading of Scripture, even when they were part of the lectionary for that day. But for many people — and for all of us at various points in our lives — expressing our sorrow to God is not only psychologically necessary but also theologically appropriate. Without these cries, Billman and Migliore argue, "there is no recognition of the real bondage and alienation of present reality . . . no genuine cry for deliverance, and no openness for new acts of God's grace."[4]

But praying the psalms of lament not only allows us to express our own grief; it also allows us to share in the sorrow of God's people elsewhere in the world. I have to admit that I, like many people, tend to pass over these psalms, feeling often that they are too depressing. I prefer the joyful psalms that express our delight at God's deliverance. But one day, while reading Psalm 44 as appointed in the common lectionary, I realized that I was reading a national lament. There the psalmist complains that though "we have not forgotten you, or been false to your covenant," still "you have broken us in the haunt of jackals, and covered us with deep darkness" (vv. 17, 19). Then he goes on to say, "Because of you we are being killed all day long, and accounted as sheep for the slaughter" (v. 22). As it happened, that very day there was an article in the newspaper that recounted the experience of women's struggle for survival amid the ethnic strife in Burundi. One woman had confessed to the reporter, "We consider ourselves sheep. . . . We have to follow all the decisions of the politicians."[5] In praying the lament of Psalm 44, I was in effect — without realizing it — crying out along with these women (over 80 percent of whom are Christians) over their apparent abandonment by their government (and, they surely felt, by God).

The practice of confession, then, can be broadened to include not only the declaration of our own failings but also the expression of our corporate sense of need for God's grace. Often we come to worship not only burdened with a sense of our sin but also sorrowing over some deep need or grief. As the traditional Anglican prayer book has it, we feel that "there is no health in us." Confession, remember, is a corporate practice in which we *together* express our need to God. So this

4. Kathleen D. Billman and Daniel L. Migliore, *Rachel's Cry: Prayer of Lament and Rebirth of Hope* (Cleveland: United Church Press, 1999), p. 126.

5. Ann M. Simmons, "Tribal Strife Is Set Aside for Survival in Burundi," *Los Angeles Times*, Sunday, 24 October 1999, p. A-18.

awareness is never simply a private one. This is a polity that encourages a shared awareness of our needs — which is the reason why many services include a time to voice or write down prayer concerns. Christians come together, as Paul says, to "bear one another's burdens, and in this way . . . fulfill the law of Christ" (Gal. 6:2). Thus the practice of worship includes activities in which this expression of need and mutual sharing of burdens is obligatory. In this way the liturgy has the potential of shaping us into people who know how to lament.

The Liturgy Joins Us into a New Community

All the actions of worship center on the pivotal fact of Christ's reconciling life and death. For many traditions, this comes into special focus in the Eucharist, where Christ's death is represented, but it is also celebrated in the reading and preaching of the Word, where Christ's life and teaching are set forth. These actions have as their goal to create a new community of people, joined by the Spirit with Christ and each other. When people kneel at the altar to receive communion, there are no national boundaries, no social classes, no ethnic barriers. As an old hymn puts it, "The ground is level at the foot of the cross." Paul's teaching in Ephesians 2 acknowledges that though differences may still exist, Christ has made all believers into one new community, one new body (v. 16). In this new unity, these differences can enrich rather than divide us.

Paul goes on to say that in this new community we are no longer strangers, but fellow citizens and "members of the household of God" (2:19). The result of this new community, Paul says in chapter 4, is that all the many gifts given to each individual are now used in a new corporate undertaking: the building up of the body of Christ (4:7, 11-12). Gifts and graces are no longer the privileged possessions of individuals and families, but common possessions whose purpose is the strengthening of community.

To my mind, the practice that best exemplifies this is our "eating and drinking" together the body and blood of Christ in the form of the bread and the wine. Recently, through participation in the ancient Corpus Christi celebration — the medieval feast of the "Body of Christ" — I have come to a renewed appreciation for what Catholics call the "'real presence' of Christ." Of course, the doctrine of the "real presence" has been much disputed since its inception during the Middle Ages. But beneath all the philosophical speculations of "accidents and substance," which most medieval worshipers didn't understand anyway, lies a very important notion: This common meal is the actual locus of Christ's continuing presence among his people. The assertion of Christ's real presence — however this is precisely understood — is a theological reality rather than an abstract or a metaphysical notion. And, interestingly, in one way or another — whether by a literal, spiritual, or remembered presence — Christians of all kinds feel that Christ is alongside them in a special way in this part of worship. I find it telling that when we leave someone for a while, we express the desire to "keep in touch." This means not only that we will remember each other but also that in some physical and tangible way we will stay together. Communion is the physical way that Christ stays with us, and we stay with him — it is the way that God has provided for us to keep in touch.

Just as we commonly say in our efforts to stay in touch with people — through letters, phone calls, and e-mails — "I'm looking forward to seeing you again," so in this worship practice we anticipate a reunion with Christ (and indeed with all believers who have gone before us). Communion is what the ancient fathers called the "Antepast of Heaven," the foretaste of what is to come. The Eucharistic meal recalls the Passover, when the Israelites celebrated their deliverance from Egypt; it looks back to the Last Supper, when Christ spoke of his body being given for us; but it also anticipates the great marriage supper of the Lamb — when the bride of Christ, this new community, is married to its Lord. Notice how this action resonates with our everyday actions of making and keeping human relationships fresh through sharing meals, recalling past celebrations, anticipating future reunions, and so on. Some scholars believe that the fourth petition of the Lord's Prayer — "Give us today our daily bread" — really means "Give us today the bread of the future age." Athanasius, the fourth-century church father, said, "Again the Lord says of himself: 'I am the living bread that came down from heaven.' [In the Lord's Prayer] he taught us ... to ask in the present age for ... the bread to come, of which we have the first-fruits in the present life when we partake of the flesh of the Lord."[6] Bread and wine, the most common of food and drink, are transformed into an anticipation of the heavenly feast.

What other cultural institution, what political structure, can teach us to see in our meals together a possibility — even a taste — of a future without boundaries and divisions? In this central act, Christians remember and represent the Lord Jesus until he comes — they keep in touch. But this meal not only represents a different polity; it also enables this to become a reality by the spiritual nourishment that it provides — something that no human meal can do. As the pastor says when distributing the elements, "This is the body of Christ, the bread of heaven." And as Calvin understood, in this act, in some mysterious way, we are joined to Christ by the Spirit.

In the Liturgy We Honor God's Material Creation

Throughout this discussion we have emphasized that worship is a set of practices — human actions and words. The miracle of worship is that ordinary actions like shaking hands, bowing heads, singing, and speaking words can become vehicles of the presence of God — they are made into prayers, blessing, and instruction. God is willing to take our common actions and words, bless them, and multiply their effects. Similarly, worship incorporates the most ordinary physical elements of our daily lives and elevates them into the architecture of the Kingdom of God. As Christ changed water to wine for a wedding feast and blessed the bread beside the sea and distributed it to the many gathered there, so, in worship, we take water, bread, and wine and declare a new creation.

6. From *De Incarnatione,* quoted in Geoffrey Wainwright, *Eucharist and Eschatology* (Akron, Ohio: Order of St. Luke Publishing, 2002), p. 39.

Nowhere is this clearer than in the central act of the Eucharist. There we take the most common of foods, as we noted, and bless them — and, miracle of miracles, God takes these common actions and these simple elements and uses them to bless us. This transformative act underlines the fact that worship embraces the material creation that God is in the process of renewing. In accepting our embodied practices and the humble elements of the Lord's Supper and making them into sacrifices of prayer and praise, worship becomes a parable — even an instance — of the redemptive work of God in the New Creation. Here the polity of worship must be seen to include our relationship with the created order — what might be called the economics of worship. The Kingdom of God, this new polity into which we are being introduced, has to do with the whole creation and the whole human being.[7] Perhaps this is why Jesus became angry when the temple was used for personal gain or the defrauding of widows (Mark 11:17; 12:40). Worship represents a transformed material and economic order. In the Eucharist, the creation, which is itself a divine gift, is taken up in all its materiality into the cosmic story of salvation. Nowhere is the two-way movement of worship we have emphasized more evident. Just as Christ came down into the world and then returned to God after the Resurrection, so God's good gift of creation comes (down) to us as a gift, a grace, which we in turn ask God to bless and offer up to him in gratitude.

Whether or not we believe that the bread is literally transformed by the dedicatory prayer is not the central point. In offering up the elements, we represent Christ's resurrection and, ultimately, *the resurrection of the created order.* The elements become a sign of the sanctification of the earth and its eventual destiny, just as they are also a sign of our own sanctification and our own resurrection. As we repeat in many liturgies of the Eucharist, "Christ has died;/Christ has risen;/ Christ is coming again."

This element of the polity of worship has broad implications. For one thing, the making of common earthly elements into spiritual

---

7. See Wainwright, *Eucharist and Eschatology,* p. 73.

signs speaks of the fact that there is no spirituality without the earth, just as there is no sanctification without the body. Our responsibility for caring for the earth, as for our bodies, follows from this. But then, finally, as I argued in the last chapter, there is no sanctification or spirituality without transformed patterns of perception that allow us to see Christ in the elements, and to see through this created order to the heavenly Jerusalem that it will one day become.

The new global Christian community is made up of citizens of another, heavenly polis. But this final element of our polity makes us realize that this heavenly community is also decidedly this-worldly. The incarnation of Christ that we represent in the communion reminds us that these worlds are linked, and that the only passage to that other world is through this earth and this body, not apart from them.

AS WE HAVE SEEN, the liturgy allows us to become a community of hospitality, of reconciliation and love, of lament and longing for wholeness, and finally of unity with each other and the created earth.

Throughout this book I have spoken about the challenge presented by the cultural (and creational) context of worship. This world not only embodies the sphere of our discipleship; it also represents, we have said, a constant threat to faithful worship. While the work of Christ and its triumph in the resurrection speak of the potential renewal of this order, they also express the condemnation of its self-seeking and pride. J. J. von Allmen notes that even in baptism the church has not been able to free itself entirely from the disorder of this world: "This world which it has condemned and which, pardoned, has been restored to it, can become a threat to Christian worship."[8] All that Christian worship expresses about the polity that informs the corporate life of Christians can be undone at any time through conformity to the demands of this world order (Rom. 12:2). It is at this point that the dramatic quality of the Christian calling comes to clearest expression. When we walk out the church door, we do not leave behind the responsibilities of faith; we begin a critical engage-

8. von Allmen, *Worship: Its Theology and Practice,* p. 46.

ment with them. The question at every moment is whether we will allow these practices to form our responses to family and colleagues and the strangers we meet, whether our projects will bear the mark of the reconciliation and community that we have celebrated in our worship practices. Will worship be a transformative force in our lives, or will the world around us press us into its own little mold? Will our lives be shaped by our worship, or will they deny what we confess?

Conclusion

There is an ancient Aramaic prayer embedded in the New Testament that has become part of our contemporary worship language: Maranatha (see Rev. 22:20). The form may be imperative, making it a kind of prayer, as it is usually translated: "Come, Lord Jesus!" This is an interesting prayer because, according to theologian Geoffrey Wainwright, it was probably placed at the beginning of the early Christian liturgies. In this form it was a prayer for Christ to be present in the earthly worship service it preceded, but it was also an (implicit) prayer for Christ's return, as appears to be the case in Revelation: "Please, Lord, come soon!" But Wainwright proposes further that the prayer might also be in the present perfect, and thus could mean "The Lord is here!"[9] The ambiguity is itself instructive, because the very presence of the Lord — hidden, as it were, under these simple forms of worship — is itself an anticipation of the glorious and visible return of Christ. This future event is the goal both of our polity and of our worship.

In the meantime, these practices of worship — humdrum as they sometimes can be — are essential as sites of the glory refracted from that future event, as rehearsals for that chorus, as strength for the journey, and much else. And for us they are the primary place provided for the reform of our distorted desires and the re-orientation of our disordered longings. They are the unique locus for the transformation of our habits into the likeness of this new polity. A Christian

---

9. Wainwright, *Eucharist and Eschatology,* p. 73.

theology of worship is not adequate if it does not stress that people who worship relate to God, each other, and the world differently. They not only have different views about the world, but actually act (and react) differently from those not formed in this way. Worship that is adequate to this vision has as its goal that people might say today what was said of the early Christians: "Behold how they love one another!"

SUGGESTIONS FOR FURTHER READING

Kathleen D. Billman and Daniel L. Migliore. *Rachel's Cry: Prayer of Lament and Rebirth of Hope.* Cleveland: United Church Press, 1999.

Ron Sider. *The Scandal of the Evangelical Conscience.* Downers Grove, Ill.: InterVarsity Press, 2005.

James K. A. Smith. *Introducing Radical Orthodoxy.* Grand Rapids: Baker, 2004.

Rodney Stark. *The Rise of Christianity.* New York: HarperCollins, 2001.

Geoffrey Wainwright. *Eucharist and Eschatology.* Akron, Ohio: Order of Saint Luke Publishing, 2002.

QUESTIONS FOR DISCUSSION

1. Why do you think worship and politics have, for many Christians, become estranged?
2. Are there dangers involved in thinking about Christianity in terms of a particular kind of politics? Are there advantages?
3. Can you think of other elements of worship, other practices, that might encourage what we are calling this alternative polity?
4. Why do you think many — especially Protestant — Christians have had trouble thinking about the Eucharist (or communion) as the "real presence" of Christ?
5. Does thinking of communion as the anticipation of the heavenly banquet encourage an "otherworldly" spirituality? Why or why not?

CHAPTER 7

Conclusion:
New Forms, New Actions

Renewing the Practices of Worship

Our discussion has shown that the practices of worship are complex, that they move on many levels. Grounded in the reality of the Trinity, they seek to celebrate the believer's participation in the life of God, and they do this by stimulating a unique set of habits. The practices of worship reflect the movement of God down to us in the life of Jesus Christ, and his ascension back into heaven; they encompass our holding up empty hands to receive the grace that God offers in Christ, and in turn our offering up ourselves and our resources to God in his service; further, they reflect our movement out of the world into a sanctuary where God can speak and bless, and then back into the world in service and mission. In short, worship is a central point of integration not only of our believing and our living, but also of this world and the next. While worship involves a very complex set of relationships and a difficult array of instructions, its importance lies in the way that it embodies these in concrete forms. It is this embodiment that we consider in this final chapter.

Worship and Aesthetics: Moving Out of the Rut

It is a common complaint of contemporary people that they have trouble seeing all their activities as relating to any single purpose or goal. A widespread worry is that life seems driven and often purposeless. As a result, people cannot see worship as anything else than another distraction in the long list of activities. Here is a case where the cultural forms exercise an unfortunate influence on the worship space: the expectations of everyday life have colonized the experience of worship. Rather than placing this everyday world into a larger portrait — as Dante, for example, was able to do in his *Divine Comedy* — people today have shrunk reality to the cramped confines of their natural world. But I am arguing that worship intends to expand our imagination, to introduce us into a larger narrative in which all the constituent parts of life find their meaning. This narrative allows us, in the words of German philologist Erich Auerbach, to discern a larger "figural interpretation [of] our everyday contemporary reality."[1] Worship provides us with an experience that places the concerns of life within a larger story in such a way that God's narrative begins to shape our own.

In this concluding chapter, I will focus more intently, and I hope more practically, on the process by which these narratives coalesce. I will argue that worship is able to accomplish this integration by allowing the Spirit of God to work in believers' lives, primarily at the level of their imagination. Of course, the Spirit in worship impacts the worshiper holistically, at cognitive, volitional, and emotional levels. But I believe that there is an important sense in which worship, when it is successful, works its transformation at the level of our imagination. For the imagination is that faculty that enables us to apprehend our lives in terms of some pattern or form. By means of the imagination, the aesthetic practices of apprehending form and the practices of worship are related.

1. Erich Auerbach, *Mimesis: The Representation of Reality in Western Literature* (Princeton: Princeton University Press, 1953), pp. 48, 49.

Theologian Don Saliers describes the link in this way: "In every age and culture, the process of evangelization into faith is, at the same time, a process of being formed in a certain aesthetic — that is, into certain patterned forms of perception."[2] Worship at its best stimulates this larger vision of things — allowing worshipers to *see* the world more as God intends it. This means that the objects and actions of worship carry significant symbolic freight. They are striving to say more than they appear to say, to point beyond themselves to this larger dramatic setting.

We have seen that Christian worship throughout history has taken on symbolic elements and shaped its worship in ways that feature aesthetic forms and actions. This became important not simply for pedagogical reasons, but also for reasons of what we today call spiritual formation. We are formed in our imagination by what we see and feel as much as by what we think about. This is especially true of things which, like worship, contain large elements of mystery. In worship we enter into a deeper awareness and celebration of God's presence as much aesthetically as we do cognitively — though both are put into play. In the early church the methods of religious instruction were deeply dramatic and aesthetic — from the regular table fellowship to the baptisms on the midnight of Easter. Cardinal Godfried Danneels describes their method this way: "Their pedagogical approach was 'sensorial': participate first and experience things at an existential level in the heart of the community, and only then explain."[3]

But this can happen only if the elements of worship take appropriate shape. Just as the narrative of salvation described in Scripture takes concrete form throughout the course of the biblical story, so the narrative of worship — which derives from the disobedience of Adam and Eve, the expulsion from the Garden, the call of Abraham, the deliverance of God's people from Egypt, and so on throughout Scripture — has a form and a particular aesthetic contour. Worship necessarily

2. Don Saliers, *Worship as Theology: Foretaste of Glory Divine* (Nashville: Abingdon Press, 1994), p. 195.
3. Godfried Danneels, "Liturgy Forty Years after the Council," *America*, August 27–September 3, 2007, p. 15.

takes on specific shapes; it becomes forms and actions that ought to resonate with the forms of Scripture. As we noted in Chapter Five, the parts of worship — from the call to worship, through the service of the Word and sacrament, to the sending — are meant to reflect the concrete forms of the story of the Gospel.

But just at this point we encounter a serious problem. The form, at least in Protestant circles, has often been left to take care of itself. Protestants in the free church tradition don't think that formal aspects of worship have much significance (though one might argue that the current controversy over forms indicates that they have more power than we have recognized). This negligence implies that the form doesn't carry theological weight, that any shape or act will do so long as it communicates the story line. In fact, one might describe the Protestant pedagogical method as the reverse of that described by Cardinal Danneels above: explain first and then encourage believers to experience "sensorially." But when it comes to the form of the biblical story, we clearly do not believe that the physical shape of things is insignificant. We think the story took a pretty definite shape, even to the extent of God entering into human history, and most Christians resist tampering with this biblical story line.

The special structure of salvation history must mean that God was concerned about the forms by which revelation was experienced, and in particular about what believers saw and heard. As Hans Urs von Balthasar says of the biblical encounter of people with God, "Perception, as a fully human act of encounter, necessarily had not only to include the senses, but to emphasize them, for it is only through the senses and in them that man perceives and acquires a sensibility for the reality of the world and of Being. And, what is more, in Christianity God appears to man right in the midst of worldly reality."[4] If this is true, there is a corollary truth that relates to worship. If it is finally through the particular forms of worship that people pray or praise,

---

4. Hans Urs von Balthasar, *The Glory of the Lord: A Theological Aesthetics,* vol. 1: *Seeing the Form,* trans. Erasmo Leiva-Merikakis, ed. Joseph Fessio and John Riches (Edinburgh: T&T Clark, 1982), p. 365.

then this becomes the final mediation that is necessary for us to worship as embodied human beings. We have no access to God apart from the particular forms or styles of worship in which we practice the presence of God. Spirituality is not a free-floating reality; it necessarily takes concrete shape. As sociologist Robert Wuthnow puts this, spirituality needs "carriers," and artistic objects often serve as indispensable carriers of a person's spirituality. He concludes that "religious teachings are validated almost aesthetically, through repetition and familiarity."[5]

Thus the forms are important for the work they do in facilitating (or occasionally obstructing) worshipers' response to God's presence. Style in this sense is not something to take lightly. The question is not whether the words, actions, and objects used in worship impact worshipers, but whether what they say and show comports well or poorly with the Gospel. In worship circles one often hears the worry that "worship should not become a performance." I understand what's behind this fear: We should not seek to show off human talent in a place that is intended to evoke God's holy presence. But whether we like it or not, when dozens of people gather together and someone sings or speaks, worship necessarily has the dimension of performance. So the question is not whether we should have a performance, but whether we plan a performance that resonates with the Gospel and that attracts our affections in appropriate ways.

Similarly, people worry about an overemphasis on visual elements — whether it is art or dance or costume — fearing that these might distract from the message of the service. But when we reflect more deeply on worship events, we realize that they are inevitably visual: there are always things to look at. Again, the better question is not whether we should use visual elements, but whether our worship has a splendor that attracts or diverts our feelings toward the Gospel.

We have seen a vivid illustration of this in the last generation, during which the "carrier" of music, generated from the music of the Je-

---

5. Robert Wuthnow, *All in Sync: How Music and Art Are Revitalizing American Religion* (Berkeley and Los Angeles: University of California Press, 2003), p. 54.

sus people, did so much to revivify worship for many. Indeed, it did more than simply facilitate worship in that situation — it actually generated a revolution in the use of music in worship. But this very fact, and the power represented by this form, emphasize not only its potential but also its danger. There are those who would argue that the use of popular Christian music has taken on a life of its own, that it no longer serves the movement of the liturgy, and that its performance too often serves as an end in itself. But for better or worse, the discussion generated by the rise of what we call "praise music" illustrates that forms and styles cannot be left to take care of themselves: they must be integrated into and disciplined by the narrative of the liturgy. And, not incidentally, this phenomenon also illustrates the way in which genuine renewal in worship can impact the larger culture.

Since aesthetic experience and religious experience are so closely linked, it follows that any attempt to renew worship must also, at the same time, include a discussion of the aesthetic dimension of worship in general and the use of arts in particular. But how can a congregation concerned about these things take steps to address them in a responsible way? In what follows I propose to suggest (briefly) five steps that a congregation may take to engage in a process of renewal that is sensitive to the aesthetic dimension — and to the imagination. Whatever the style of worship to which a congregation is accustomed, something like the following steps may be useful in moving toward a renewed, Spirit-led vision of worship. These steps are premised on the thesis that worship *in itself* does not transform the worshiper or the world; only the Word of God in the power of the Spirit can do this. But the experience of God does not happen in isolation from our embodied life in the world — it needs carriers. And our engagement with the practice of worship is a critical point at which the grace and power of God can be made visible. More importantly, the prayerful process of reflection on our worship is a necessary part of faithful discipleship.

Five Steps for Renewing Worship

Reflect on the History and Character of Your Congregation

In the mid-1990s the Lilly Foundation sponsored a study on why pastors fail during their first call. One of the three major reasons was that they did not understand the character of their congregation and the way their ministry fit into that history and character. One major aspect of the personality of a congregation that I want to call attention to is the "imagination" that this group brings to worship. How do they "see" themselves?

As I see it, too much talk about church renewal proceeds on a very generic and abstract level — worship needs or lacks this or that element. It is not surprising that general suggestions often feel vague and unconvincing. The first question to ask, then, is not "What does this congregation need to do to 'spice up' worship?" but "Who are these people, and how do they understand themselves as worshipers?" One part of that is surely having members tell their stories of life in the church as a means of developing a history and a profile of that congregation. Another is to talk to them about their experience of worship. Recently I published the results of a major research project in which my students and I asked a wide variety of worshipers in Los Angeles what they understood worship to be and how the forms of worship, especially the visual, impacted them. Let me describe a little of what I discovered.[6]

I found out — not surprisingly — that for Protestant worshipers, the experience of worship has an inward and personal focus. It is a personal encounter with God that takes place within (which, I believe, is why we have learned to close our eyes at the most intimate points of worship — a practice that only dates back, as nearly as I can tell, to the Reformation). One pastor put it this way in an interview: "Worship to me means to attribute worth to God. So, worship is not singing, it's

6. See *The Senses of the Soul: Art and the Visual in Christian Worship* (Eugene, Ore.: Wipf & Stock, 2008).

not art in and of itself. . . . Those are enhancers by which we may attribute worth to God. . . . It's not about us; it's all about him. And so those things that help me — creatively or otherwise — to attribute worth to God are valuable."

Notice what comments like this imply for the form of worship. Since it is inward and personal, there can be no intrinsic connection with any external thing. External things — a song, an image, a poem — can spark this experience, but they can also block it. All of this has great implications for the kind of innovations that might be helpful in this situation. Perhaps the responses of people in your congregation would be different. Perhaps they would be more open to new things — or perhaps even more closed to them. Discovering through surveys or focus groups how they think about themselves in relation to worship, how they "imagine" their experience, is an essential step in knowing how worship might be renewed.

Review and Reflect on the Liturgy

Having reflected on the expectations that people bring to worship, the next step is to reflect on the practices of worship that the congregation has inherited. At this point it is important to ask questions like these: Why do we worship in the way that we do? What have we inherited from our tradition? Whatever style may be dominant, this review will involve tracking the theological movement of the liturgy and reflecting on how the order of the service draws people into the presence of God and what it emphasizes in the process. In this book I am arguing that all Christian worship, of whatever tradition, should include, in some form, the invitation and welcome of God to worship, the announcement and explanation of God's Word, the invitation to communion or the Eucharist, and the blessing and sending by God into the world. Members of the congregation should be urged to reflect on this fourfold movement, perhaps the theological heritage (Lutheran, Reformed, free church) it embodies and the importance of this for spiritual growth. They should spend considerable time exploring the biblical foundations and traditional shape of the worship they have inherited. Here they might ask a number of questions. What particular biblical themes do our tradition and our worship emphasize? How does our worship reflect this heritage, or, perhaps, how has it diverged from this? What is the theological movement we want to highlight?

This kind of deep reflection on the experience of worship is all too rare in our churches, which may account for much of the weakness of our worship. The reality is that what happens in worship and how we can, and do, experience God's presence are not matters of interest to scholars alone; they are important to everyone who comes through the door of the church. People will respond favorably when they are encouraged to reflect on the way in which the practices of worship currently in use facilitate (or do not facilitate) the theological movement of the service and promote a deeper experience with God. Everything that is done ought, in some way, to lend its weight to this central narrative. So the questions become these: How, and in what ways, does the order that exists enhance this movement? In what ways does it impede it? The core practices of prayer, confession, praise, Word, creed, and blessing will always be present, but they can take on a multitude of forms. But how effective are the current forms? Do the practices of our worship adequately carry the theological movement that we value? In order to fully answer this question, it will be necessary to move to the next step.

Listen to the Culture

I have been arguing that the core practices of worship represent the ordinary way in which believers are shaped by the Spirit into the likeness of Christ. Similarly, the cultural patterns that people bring with them into the worship service represent the ordinary way in which they relate to each other, express their values, and represent their world to themselves. Culture expresses, in the first instance, the limits of the possible. And the space of worship, I am arguing, is a specially defined cultural space. Just as people cannot worship in languages they do not understand, so their worship must connect in some way with their cultural values. The degree and nature of this connection will of course vary from congregation to congregation, depending on the understanding of worship and the liturgical style. But reflection on this relationship is clearly necessary, if for no other reason than to avoid unconscious influences.

One of the weaknesses of current discussions of worship is the failure to connect the second step of the process with the third — that is, the biblical and theological reflection with the cultural analysis. Indeed, those who stress the importance of reflecting on the liturgy and its historical development often see little need to engage with contemporary culture, and those interested in connecting with the culture often have little interest in the historical developments of liturgy. Normally these groups sit on opposite sides of the spectrum we proposed in Chapter Three, and too often they have little to do with each other. But there is no inherent conflict between seeking to deepen our theological and traditional roots and finding wholesome ways to engage our surrounding culture. Indeed, these processes are complementary.

Since the early church, liturgy and culture have had a mutual influence on each other, and this continues to be the case. Whether we celebrate or lament contemporary culture, it does impact the way that people coming into our churches experience and relate to the world, and thus how they will engage worship. We reviewed some of the contemporary values in Chapter Five, but here let me focus on one point that was not stressed there: the fact that contemporary culture is almost entirely visually mediated. Videos, movies, TV, even cell phones and iPods mediate the world largely through images. Moreover, educational researchers tell us that 60 percent of the population are visual learners, understanding things best through images rather than through words alone. This is not to say that words are becoming unimportant or are losing their power, but that the relationship between word and image is changing. Again, whether one believes this is a good thing or a bad thing, it is a fact of the culture that must be recognized and engaged.

An interesting aspect of this visual turn in our culture is that those born in recent decades are more likely to perceive themselves as artistic or creative, or to say that the arts are important to them. Robert Wuthnow has shown that of those born in the 1970s, 66 percent say they are creative, compared with 45 percent of those born in the 1930s and only 16 percent of those born in the decade beginning in 1910.[7] In general, there is a rapidly increasing interest and involvement in the arts in the last generation. In a recent report to advertisers and marketers, Daniel Yankelovich, president of the Public Agenda Foundation, urged them to consider the importance of products that express an "aesthetic sensibility." More than half of those he surveyed rated highly "using their imaginations," and this appears to be true across generations and genders. More interesting is the trend: those who rated "having a sense of style" as extremely or very important increased from 29 percent to 36 percent from 2001 to 2006, and those wanting to express their creative side, similarly, increased from 38 percent to 46 percent. Yankelovich went on to make this recommendation: "In the retail world, consider one-of-a-kind retail environments that keep the consumer engaged by activating their artistic imagination."[8]

It is not hard to see the implications of this for music and especially for the visual dimension of worship. For contemporary worshipers, increasingly, the aesthetic dimension is important. The environment usually has been crafted to suit particular styles of worship and to reflect a specific tradition. Understanding this baseline is a necessary starting point in worship planning. But the next step is to recognize that the movement of the service involves various visual and dramatic events. Even sermons, litanies, and prayers have their visual dimensions. Thus the question in this case is not whether worship should be visual or creative, but *how* the visual dimension of current practices enhances or impedes worship, especially for a generation raised in a visual culture. The point here is not to suggest how this

7. Wuthnow, *All in Sync*, p. 66.
8. Yankelovich Report, *Monitor Minute,* 5 December 2006.

connection should be made — though the suggested readings at the end of the chapter make some helpful proposals — but to insist that these conversations take place as part of the process of renewal.

Any conversation about culture must surely be cross-generational; indeed, in matters of culture our children often become our teachers. Clearly, those raised in a media-rich environment have a wholly different take on media than their parents do. For them, media have become a much more normal — and all-pervasive — part of their lives. Here we need to listen to our children — not simply because we want to keep them engaged in church, but because they have been raised in a different world, and their worship experience will need to connect with that world.

Release the Poets

The next step may be a surprise to some. But it is a growing conviction of many that an essential step in the process of renewal is to once again make the space of the church into a center of creativity and imagination. The brief historical comments earlier in the book have reminded us that vibrant worship and cultural innovation have often been correlated. Indeed, in the medieval period the best artists and poets subscribed to what was called a *theologica poetica*. This theory held that the highest artistic works of all time, especially as this was embodied in imagery and poetry that engaged the imagination and the affections, could be a significant bearer of theological truth. While many religious people initially opposed this idea, it served as an important creative stimulus for people like Dante and Luca Signorelli (who was a critical influence on Michelangelo). This openness to culture made it possible for the church of the Middle Ages to be the cradle for all the major arts — the visual arts, music, and drama. Moreover, as I argued in Chapter Five, the genius of narrative is that it provides a figural interpretation of everyday life. If this is so, then the forms of worship that will best stimulate such a vision of life will themselves be figural and emotionally striking.

With the exception of music, the arts and worship have gone their

149

separate ways in the last few hundred years. But there are increasing signs that this is changing; churches and Christian groups are increasingly encouraging artists and art-making. Given the nature of our culture and the openness of the younger generation in particular to the arts, a necessary part of the process of renewal will surely include encouraging all forms of the arts. On the basis of extensive research, Robert Wuthnow has shown that there is a correlation between involvement in the arts and interest in spirituality. Furthermore, this spiritual interest isn't casual or shallow. Those most interested in art and aesthetic experience are more likely to be deeply interested in religious traditions. As we noted earlier, Wuthnow hypothesizes that this is because spirituality demands "carriers," and aesthetic forms are natural carriers of religious meaning — as is evident from previous periods of Christian history.[9] As I have argued, forms or practices of worship are not optional extras but essential bearers of spiritual meanings. The ordinary way to deep encounters with God is through the forms and material shapes of our shared worship experience. If they are not shaped in lovely and striking ways, how can God be glorified? How can we be nurtured?

We noted above the special connection between aesthetics and religious experience. Both involve the special use of the imagination in opening our consciousness to transcendent patterns and to the possibility of an encounter with God. Being open to an artwork, to an experience of hearing an artistic word, has deep similarities to standing before God and being open to hearing a word from our creator.

For this connection to be appropriately and fruitfully made, churches must be open to the artistic gifts in their midst — indeed, they must determine to nurture these gifts. I am amazed at how churches find ways to use some gifts and not others. Business, technical, and catering skills are particularly in demand in many churches, while the artists in their midst are mostly overlooked. Especially in Protestant churches, art is considered a kind of hobby and certainly not essential to the spiritual life of the congregation. These attitudes

9. Wuthnow, *All in Sync*.

150

must change. Ways must be found to encourage and nurture those gifted artistically so that they can use these gifts to the glory of God.

There are a number of practical steps the church leadership can take to this end. They can encourage development of an artists' network, through which artists can share their work and support each other. They can also set aside spaces in the church for artists to perform and exhibit their work. This doesn't necessarily mean that artists should be immediately included in the worship service, however important that might be later on. The initial goal should be to find a way to release and encourage artistic gifts and to nurture artists as believers. They need help in understanding how their artistic gifts relate to their faith journey, and how these have been related throughout the history of the church.

Re-imagine Worship

When these steps have been taken — but not, I believe, before — then it is time to reflect again on the liturgy. When the congregation understands its liturgical and theological tradition, when it has reflected deeply on the cultural situation with its assets and liabilities, and when those with artistic gifts have been nurtured, then it is possible to revisit the liturgy and pray for the touch of the Spirit. Perhaps this is the time to form a committee on worship and the arts that is broadly representative of the congregation (in age, gender, ethnicity, and talents). Along with the pastor and the board, this group could help the congregation explore again their experience of worship. The group could lead the congregation in reflecting on the environment of worship — the use of space, lighting, color, sound, and so on — to discover ways in which art and aesthetic elements could be used to enhance the movement of the liturgy.

Here one must seek a balance between pastoral sensitivity and openness to the Spirit. More important than any particular result is the process that the congregation undertakes. For in worship-planning the goal is not necessarily a particular tangible outcome so much as the growth resulting from a shared process of reflection and prayer. On the other hand, one sees often in the history of the church a correlation between openness to the Spirit and visible creativity. Certainly we can hope and pray that we see signs that young men are seeing visions and old men are dreaming dreams, which Peter (in Acts 2) predicts will be a sign of the Spirit's presence.

Conclusion

Worship practices that take their cue from Scripture will show that human life points toward a future that is richly aesthetic and dramatic. The book of Revelation reminds us that worship forms are part of an expansive dramatic vision — they anticipate the heavenly vision of people of every tribe and tongue and nation gathering before the throne.[10] In that grand experience of worship, God's people will celebrate their collective stories. Indeed, the vision of heaven given to John in Revelation — where he was "in the Spirit on the Lord's day" (Rev. 1:10) — represents a kind of summation of biblical narratives. In fact, this "collection" of narratives is a main characteristic of John's vision on Patmos, which is framed in terms of worship. The best biblical stories have a certain minimalist tendency — a focus on particular actions and characters. But in the Revelation of John, the threads of biblical narrative are woven together into a complex vision of God dwelling in a new creation with his people. Notice that this is not a denial of the preceding stories but their climax; it does not analyze the stories so much as collect them.

This leads us to a final example of the many-leveled movement of worship. We have emphasized the twofold character of worship — that it represents God's movement down to people and their active response to this. Worship also represents a combination of retreat from life and its re-formation. Worship brings together the movement of

---

10. I have elaborated this vision of the future in the conclusion of *The Earth Is God's: A Theology of American Culture* (Eugene, Ore.: Wipf & Stock, 1996), from which this section borrows.

time and the quiet stillness of a timeless vision of God into a single integrated whole. It is not accidental that more hymns are found in the book of Revelation than in any other biblical book except the Psalms, for it is a vision of a time when creation itself, along with redeemed humanity, seems constantly to break into song. Symbols — bowls and trumpets, scrolls and seals — crowd in on one another; visual, dramatic, and musical spectacles are layered on top of one another. As might be expected, our analytic and cognitive mode of reflecting has largely smothered this vitality, replacing its pulsating life with charts and principles. But this cumulative vision cannot so easily be suppressed. It concentrates and focuses the biblical stories, suggesting an aesthetic display of meaning in a final and altogether new creation. It is this new creation that we celebrate — indeed, that we shape and sustain — in our worship.

In a way, we have come back to the point where we began. In the introduction, I quoted Samuel Balentine, who suggests that worship constitutes an activity of world construction.[11] The practices of worship together prod our imagination to see another world in the midst of this one. Now we can propose that such an imagination, empowered by the Spirit, enables believers to actually live in terms of this new creation. When a family bows their heads to pray before a meal, they are construing the act of eating together as a sacramental event. Their meal takes on symbolic depth. It recalls the meal wherein food and drink actually became the body and blood of Christ; it anticipates the great feast, when people from all nations will sit and celebrate the Lamb that was slain. When God's people pray at the beginning of the day and leave their homes, they enter a city that itself can be transparent to the purposes of God in the New Jerusalem. Indeed, they have the imagination to see through the imperfections and pain of their earthly city to a city whose builder and maker is God. Most of all, worship's vision gives them hope to go out and work until, as William Blake says, by God's grace, "we have built Jerusalem."

11. Samuel Balentine, *The Torah's Vision of Worship* (Minneapolis: Fortress Press, 1999), p. 34.

SUGGESTIONS FOR FURTHER READING

B. Beit-Hallahmi. "Religion as Art and Identity." Pp. 171-88 in *Psychology of Religion: Personalities, Problems, Possibilities,* ed. H. N. Malony. Pasadena, Calif.: Integration Press, 1991.

Nancy Chinn. *Spaces for Spirit: Adorning the Church.* Chicago: Liturgy Training Publications, 1998.

Catherine Kapikian. *Art in the Service of the Sacred.* Ed. Kathy Black. Nashville: Abingdon Press, 2006.

Quentin Schultze. *High-Tech Worship? Using Presentational Technologies Wisely.* Grand Rapids: Baker, 2004.

Calvin Institute of Christian Worship (Web site)

QUESTIONS FOR DISCUSSION

1. Discuss what catches your attention in the environment in which you worship. What does this mean to you?
2. Can you think of any time that a visual experience has made a deep spiritual impression on you? What about a particular work of music?
3. In what ways can biblical imagery, parables, and stories be interpreted in the worship setting?
4. What problems are involved in using an unusual art form in worship? What positive or negative experience have you had with such forms?
5. What are some of the possible things that worship planners might learn from "the youth culture"?